Trust in God

Trust in God

The Christian Life
and the *Book of Confessions*

David W. Johnson

Geneva Press
Louisville, Kentucky

First edition
Published by Geneva Press
Louisville, Kentucky

13 14 15 16 17 18 19 20 21 22—10 9 8 7 6 5 4 3 2 1

Book design by Sharon Adams
Cover design by Dilu Nicholas
Cover illustration: abstract background © Jelena Veskovic/istockphoto.com

Library of Congress Cataloging-in-Publication Data

Johnson, David W.
   Trust in God : the christian life and the Book of confessions / David W. Johnson.
-- First edition.
      pages cm.
   Includes bibliographical references and index.
   ISBN 978-0-664-50302-4 (alk. paper)
   1. Presbyterian Church (U.S.A.). Book of confessions.   2. Presbyterian Church (U.S.A.).—Creeds.   3. Reformed Church—Creeds.   4. Christian life—Presbyterian authors.   I. Title.
   BX8969.5.J64   2013
   248.4'85137—dc23

                                                                                              2012033215

Most Geneva Press books are available at special quantity discounts when purchased in bulk by corporations, organizations, and special-interest groups. For more information, please e-mail SpecialSales@GenevaPress.com.

Contents

Acknowledgments

I would like to express my gratitude to the following people:

My colleagues at Austin Presbyterian Theological Seminary, many of whom read portions of the manuscript and offered valuable suggestions. I would especially like to express my gratitude to Theodore Wardlaw, the President of Austin Presbyterian Theological Seminary, and Allan Cole, the Academic Dean.

Ellen Babinsky, who read the entire manuscript and provided a detailed critique that enabled me to strengthen my work considerably.

Tammy Wiens, who gave constant encouragement and insightful critique at every stage of this work's development.

Jane C. Johnson, to whom I am married, who also read and responded to the entire manuscript. Her responses and sharp editorial eye have been invaluable.

Donald McKim, who suggested I undertake this project and who has been constantly supportive and remarkably patient as it has developed.

I would like to dedicate this book to the Presbyterian Church (U.S.A.) in the hope that it will help to strengthen our faith and our witness in challenging times.

Introduction

The *Book of Confessions* came into being a half-century ago. How to use it is still something of an enigma. The documents making up the *Book of Confessions* were declared to be "subordinate standards" (*Book of Order* F-2.02) that "serve to strengthen personal commitment and the life and witness of the community of believers" (*BO* F-2.01).

Such strengthening, if it is to happen at all, must depend on the contents of the confessions being known. An unread *Book of Confessions* has no more power to strengthen personal commitment and the life of the community than an unread Bible. Many of the difficulties people experience in reading the Bible also surface when they read the *Book of Confessions*. Just as with the Bible, the *Book of Confessions* is more like a library than a single book. The various creeds, confessions, and catechism were written at different times under different circumstances to address different issues. Only the Confession of 1967 and the Brief Statement of Faith can be considered to be contemporary in any sense. This means that today's Christians will have some difficulty even understanding them, let alone applying them.

A knowledge of the history can help, of course, and current editions of the *Book of Confessions* contain brief accounts of how and why the confessions came about. Knowing the historical context of the confessions can help one understand both their intent and their limitations. The meaning of the confessions, however, cannot be restricted to their own times. They also speak to us today in ways that transcend their times. They are more than historical curiosities; they provide guidance to the church.

In this book, I want to examine the Christian spiritual life using the *Book of Confessions* as a guide. While this will certainly require some attention to history, my primary intent is not historical. Rather, I want to show how the

Book of Confessions can speak to contemporary Christians about what it means to *be* a Christian, and how one goes about living a Christian life. I want to do this particularly to help members of Presbyterian congregations, and the pastors who serve those congregations, understand what the Reformed tradition teaches.

I do not intend this book to be limited to Presbyterians, however. There are many branches of the Reformed tradition—the World Communion of Reformed Churches lists 230 churches in 108 countries worldwide.[1] Even beyond this, Reformed churches are a part of the church universal, and they speak to it and learn from it. Consequently, in some sense I am speaking to all who are interested in Christian spirituality and who might benefit from engaging the Reformed tradition on any level that seems appropriate to them.

The first three chapters of the book form an introduction to Christian spirituality. The first chapter looks at the words we use, the second explores the relationship between spirituality and human development, and the third provides a sketch of the Reformed tradition as it relates to spirituality.

The second half of the book goes deeper into the Reformed understanding of spirituality, including spiritual practices and disciplines, under the rubrics of faith, love, and hope. Finally, three appendixes give some concrete guidelines for engaging in Bible reading, prayer, and confession—the three central spiritual disciplines of the Reformed tradition.

This book, then, is an invitation to learn that Reformed Christianity is not simply a historical tradition or a theological orientation, but a way of life. It is a way of life that celebrates the majesty of God's grace, the paradox of freedom in obedience, and the determination to make God's world increasingly conformed to God's will. This way of life once transformed the world. It has the power to do so again.

1

Some Words

The Vocabulary of Faith

TALKING THE WALK

Words are one of the factors that make human beings unique. We use words to communicate information, desires, and feelings. We use words to say, "I love you," and "Look out!" We rhyme words, sing words, shout words, think words, pray words. People who cannot use words are isolated and handicapped. Even if other animals communicate with sounds, and it seems undeniable that they do, no other animal seems to do the variety of things that we do with words. The world of humans is inconceivable without words.

But we have come to distrust words. We have heard too many vague promises, ambiguous truth claims, and outright lies to give unquestioned credit to a person's words. We want to see actions. "You can talk the talk, but can you walk the walk?" we ask. There are, we fear, many more talkers than walkers in our world.

Yet talking the talk is an important part of our lives, including our spiritual lives. The Word has a certain priority in the Christian faith. It was, according to the Gospel of John, in the beginning with God (John 1:1). It became flesh. It was full of grace and truth.

Our words are not God's word. They are, at best, a response to God's word. Nevertheless, they are important, and we need to get them right. "Faith comes from what is heard" (Rom. 10:17), Paul writes. If we do not hear, our walking, should it occur at all, will be aimless wandering, without purpose, guidance, or direction.

The spiritual life requires words. Some of those words are from the Bible. Some of them are from the long history of the church's reflection on the Bible—the material such as theological treatises, creeds, and confessions, as well as poetry, music, and artwork, that forms the church's tradition. Some of them are from our surrounding culture. Some of them are from our minds and hearts.

I want to begin this study by considering some of the words and phrases that occur over and over in talking about Christian spirituality. I want to be as clear as I can about what these words mean and how they are used, particularly in the *Book of Confessions*. This is not just a matter of speaking cogently and carefully. It is also a part of the walking, for our words will guide and illuminate our walking. So we must begin with some words.

Speaking of God

How do we talk about God? Our words are drawn from the world around us. How can they be appropriate for God if God is the other, absolutely beyond our world?

People realized quite early that speaking of God required a special use of language, usually called *analogical*, in which words are used in similar but not identical ways. For example, consider these sentences:

> This is a good apple.
> My dog is a good dog.
> Mary is a good person.
> God is good.

The common element in these sentences is the word *good*, but the *good* does not mean the same thing in each sentence. The apple is good because it is crisp, fresh, juicy, and has no worms hiding within. That is not true of my dog (except possibly for the worms). My good dog is obedient, friendly, trustworthy, and reluctant to bite. Mary, the good person, is honest, fair, open-minded, and warmhearted. What *good* means is that we have standards or tests for whatever we are talking about, and whatever we are talking about fits or conforms to those standards.

But are there standards for the goodness of God? There are, and the Bible is full of them: "For you, O Lord, are good and forgiving, abounding in steadfast love to all who call on you" (Ps. 86:5). God's goodness, according to this verse, is demonstrated by God's forgiveness and love. But what do *forgiveness* and *love* mean? Are God's forgiveness and love like human forgiveness and love? Yes they are, or we would simply not know what we are talking about. Yet God's forgiveness and love must be more than ours. For one thing, they are eternal, while our forgiveness and love are variable and transient. Our talking about God is analogical—we can say true things about God with human words, for there is a similarity between human qualities and divine qualities. But God will always be greater than anything our human words can say, because God is greater than we are. We can say true things about God, but we can never express God's true greatness.

In our time, our ways of talking about God have been strongly criticized. In the Apostles' and Nicene Creeds, for example, the persons of the Trinity are called *Father, Son,* and *Holy Spirit.* Feminist theologians have objected that this gives a false picture of God as a male and thus makes masculinity an attribute of the divine. They have suggested returning to language of God as Mother, as some in the church did in ancient and medieval times, or speaking of the Trinity in gender-neutral terms, such as *Creator, Redeemer,* and *Sustainer.*

To suggest that masculinity or femininity is an attribute of the divine is a form of idolatry. God has no gender. The word *Father*, when used of God, speaks of a relationship, as does the word *Son.* This relationship is similar in some ways to, but infinitely more than, the relationship between a parent and a child.[1]

THE STARTING POINT

Christian spirituality has its origin in this basic affirmation: *There is another.* This is not distinctively or exclusively Christian. It can certainly be affirmed by adherents of Judaism, Islam, certain forms of Hinduism, and people who do not have any religious affiliation at all.

Yet certain things are ruled out from the beginning. In the face of this basic affirmation, the spiritual path cannot simply be the road to self-realization, greater authenticity, or increased sensitivity to what is real and what is not. The spiritual path must somehow be the path to or with the other.

Christian spirituality moves from its origin to a second affirmation: *The relationship between this other and myself is the crucial factor in my life.* This is not an inevitable consequence of the basic affirmation. It is perfectly possible to believe that there is another, what is typically called *God*, and yet deny that God has anything to do with us. God might be the creator who left the creation to fend for itself. God might be as far removed from us as a distant galaxy. God might not care at all about us. God might, in fact, be our enemy. Such beliefs make Christian spirituality impossible. If God is not involved with us, if God is absent from our life except as a far-distant creator, there is no reason to be involved with God. All we can do is get on with life as best we can. If God is our enemy, we had best avoid God altogether.

Only the two affirmations taken together start us along the spiritual path: *There is another. The relationship between this other and myself is the crucial factor in my life.* This is the path of seeking and finding, of longing and fulfillment, of obedience or disobedience, of error and redemption, of going out and coming home. It is the path to God. It is the path with God. It is also the path beset by demons, including—especially including—the demons in oneself. It is the path that distinguishes between solitude and abandonment, prayer and merely wishing, self-surrender and selfish willfulness. It is the path of paradox, for on it one finds freedom in obedience, life in dying, and supreme reality in that which cannot be seen or felt or tasted or touched. It is the path of sacrifice, of privation, even of pain, and yet of supreme blessing. It is the path that can only be explored by the walking. Any mapping in advance is provisional; any report by other travelers is approximate.

GOD

Who, then, is the other? Who is the one whose relationship forms the crucial factor in my life?

God is the Other—other than ourselves, other than our world, other than the entire cosmos. God is, in a phrase often used by theologians, wholly other.

God's otherness can be frightening. The people of the Bible who encountered God found these events terrifying. The people of Israel, gathered on Mt. Sinai, said to Moses, "You speak to us, and we will listen; but do not let God speak to us, or we will die" (Exod. 20:19). Much later, on another mountain, the apostle Peter was terrified into virtual incoherence by the sight of the transfigured Jesus (Mark 9:2–13, with parallels in Matthew and Luke). "Our God comes and does not keep silence," the psalmist exclaims. "Before him is a devouring fire, and a mighty tempest all around him" (Ps. 50:3). One does well to respect devouring fires; one's life might hang in the balance.

But God's otherness is in truth the highest grace. Only the one who is other could be present with us and to us and for us wherever we might go. We can travel from the United States to the North Pole, or from the earth to the stars, and not get any farther from God—or any closer to God. Our distance from God is immeasurable and infinitesimal. God is infinitely beyond us in order to be infinitely close to us.

Our attempts to say who God is, or what God is, or even *that* God is, will always be marked by such paradoxes, for if God is so far beyond us, God is certainly beyond the expressive power of our language. But keeping silent is no option. God commands us to speak. God also helps us speak. This is God's way. To turn St. Augustine's prayer into a declarative, God gives what God commands.[2] We find this out, however, only in the living of it. As an idea or a concept, it holds little comfort.

If the "how" of speaking about God necessitates the use of analogical language, what does that language say? What can we say of God, and on what basis?

The answer to this question brings us to another paradox, perhaps the ultimate paradox in the life of a Christian. In order to know the God who is God, the God who is wholly and completely other, you have to know a particular human being who lived in the ancient Near East. He was an itinerant rabbi, the son of a carpenter and a peasant woman, who was born under mysterious circumstances, whose life was obscure until the last few months (or possibly years) before his death, who was executed as a criminal, and whose followers believed and taught that he returned to life. In this unlikely place through this unlikely person, you can gaze into the eyes of God.

JESUS CHRIST

You have to meet Jesus in the concrete. Jesus is not Everyman. Jesus is not some universal symbol of the good, or the holy, or the highest human aspiration. Jesus is not an idea or an ideal. Jesus is not an abstraction. Jesus is not a dream or a fantasy. Jesus is not an artifact of the collective imagination.

Above all, Jesus is not you. Jesus is the other—that is one of the marks of his divinity. He is the stranger. You will not know him on sight. You have to get to know him. He can and will become your friend. He is already your brother. But he is not to be found in the vague twilight of symbol or fantasy. Seek him in the daylight.

You find Jesus, not *in* Scripture, but *through* Scripture. Scripture could hardly contain him. It can only point to him. The sum total of words about Jesus is not Jesus. The sum total of stories about Jesus is not Jesus. But through the words, through the stories, Jesus meets us and calls us and claims us. We encounter Jesus' wisdom through his teachings. We encounter Jesus' power through his extraordinary deeds, his "miracles." We encounter Jesus' compassion through his self-offering. When Jesus says to his disciples, "Follow me," he also says it to us. When he says to the woman caught in adultery, "Neither do I condemn you" (John 8:10), he also says it to us. When he says to his disciples, "You shall be my witnesses" (Acts 1:8), he also says it to us.

There is more to say about Scripture—what it is, what it is not, how to read it, how to use it in living. We will return to that in chapter 4. For now, this is the crucial point: Through Scripture you will meet Jesus. You will learn to recognize him. You will learn to recognize God in him. Then you will find yourself recognizing him everywhere.

HOLY SPIRIT

There is a third, who is also other: The Holy Spirit. The Nicene Creed calls her " Lord," as it calls Jesus "Lord," and says that she gives life, speaks through prophets, and worthy of worship (*BC* 1.3). This Spirit is with you, in you, and around you right now, as the intimate presence of God. But this Spirit is also the other, and so is not limited to the one single time and place where you are. She is also above you, in a high and holy place, at one with the Father and the Son.

We read in Romans 8:9 that the Spirit dwells within us. But the Spirit is God, and our hearts cannot contain her. We cannot possess the Holy Spirit, even in our hearts. The Spirit will possess us, taking us captive in order to set us free—another paradox. But it's the only way.

The Spirit obviously has something to do with spirituality. True spirituality is aware of the Spirit, open to the Spirit, responsive to the Spirit, submissive to the Spirit. It is never in control of the Spirit.

The sovereignty of the Holy Spirit is a constant theme in the *Book of Confessions*. The Spirit is one with the Father and the Son, and the Spirit's work of redemption is one with the work of the Father and the Son. The Heidelberg Catechism stresses both of these teachings:

> Q. 53. What do you believe concerning "the Holy Spirit"?
>
> A. First, that, with the Father and the Son, he is equally eternal God; second, that God's Spirit is also given to me, preparing me through a true faith to share in Christ and all his benefits, that he comforts me and will abide with me forever. (*BC* 4.054)

The Reformed tradition views any attempt to separate the Holy Spirit from the Father and the Son with extreme hostility. It does not allow any new revelation through the Spirit apart from the revelation through the Son. Neither will it allow any temporal distinction: There is no new age of the Spirit or any new era or dispensation of the Spirit in Reformed theology.

TRINITY

Father, Son, and Holy Spirit are three, but only one God. To use the theological vocabulary that developed in the early church, they are three *persons*, but a single *substance*.

Many of the confessions deal with this issue. The Nicene Creed (really the Constantinopolitan Creed[3]) is the result of over a half-century of acrimonious debate about the divinity of and the relationship between Father, Son, and Holy Spirit. In its present form, it decisively and explicitly affirms the divinity of Father, Son, and Holy Spirit. All the other documents in the *Book of Confessions* (with the exception of the Apostles' Creed, which had its origin before the Council of Nicea, although it evolved over many centuries) either explicitly affirm this formulation of the doctrine of the Trinity or presuppose it.

Christian theology often speaks of a certain quality or activity in relation to only one of the persons of the Trinity. "Father, Son, and Holy Spirit" is sometimes replaced by "Creator, Redeemer, and Sustainer," for example, in an effort to avoid language that implies a gender. The Apostles' Creed speaks in this way: The Father creates heaven and earth; the Son suffers, dies, and is raised from the dead; and the Holy Spirit enables the church and its ministry. This creed, in turn, reflects the language of Scripture.

This does not mean, however, that the persons of the Trinity are ever separated from each other in being or activity. In relation to the creation, Father, Son, and Holy Spirit are always together, always active, always at work. Where one of the persons is found, the others are present. They can be distinguished from each other, but they are never separated from each other.

It is easy to lose patience with the doctrine of the Trinity. To say that God is both one and three is confusing on the face of it, and the explanations about how this can be are often convoluted and abstract. Contemporary minds tend to find it odd that one might die for one's beliefs about the Trinity, and repulsive that one might put others to death for disagreeing with one's beliefs about the Trinity. Yet that has happened many times in the history of the church.

It is important to realize, however, that the church said what it said about the Trinity and by and large has continued to say it, because that was the only way that it could do justice to all the Bible says about God. The Bible's constant affirmation is that there is only one God, but the New Testament seems both to identify Jesus of Nazareth with that God and to distinguish him from that God.[4] The reason that the doctrine of the Trinity has been so difficult throughout the history of the church is this: Either we must live with the paradoxical mystery of one-in-threeness, or we must give up something important that the Bible says about God. The choice of most of the church throughout its history has been to live with and in the paradoxical mystery.

A consequence of this mystery is that God cannot be described simply with a list of superlatives. God must also be described by relationships. The Westminster Confession of Faith begins its treatment of God with two long paragraphs, which indeed consist of a list of superlatives: "immutable, immense, eternal, incomprehensible, almighty; most wise, most holy, most free, most absolute" (*BC* 6.011–6.012). Christians understand these two paragraphs as describing the entire Godhead—the Trinity—but most Jews or Muslims could affirm very similar statements with regard to Yahweh or Allah. When the Confession turns to the Trinity, however, the language describes a series of relationships: "The Father is of none, neither begotten nor proceeding; the Son is eternally begotten of the Father; the Holy Ghost eternally proceeding from the Father and the Son" (*BC* 6.013). The names of the relationships are activities: begetting and proceeding.

God, then, is not a simple God. Relationship is at the heart of the God-head. Is this any more than (possibly) interesting information?

Human Relationships

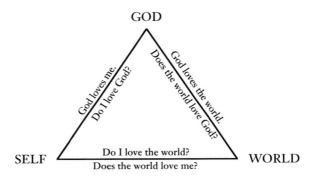

In fact, the God-in-relationship is important both for our salvation and for our identity. For salvation, the doctrine of the Trinity says, "Your Redeemer, your Savior, is God." As far as our identity is concerned, the doctrine of the Trinity tells us this: "You were made in the image of God, and that image is relational."

HUMANS

Then God said, "Let us make humankind in our image, according to our likeness; and let them have dominion over the fish of the sea, and over the birds of the air, and over the cattle, and over all the wild animals of the earth, and over every creeping thing that creeps upon the earth." So God created humankind in his image, in the image of God he created them; male and female he created them. (Gen. 1:26–27)

Who is God talking to in this passage? Who is "us"? The fifth-century theologian Augustine of Hippo maintained that "us" was the entire Trinity and "our likeness" indicated that the image in which humans were created was the image of the Trinity. Augustine found that Trinitarian image in the human mind (in the interplay of memory, understanding, and will) and the human heart (for wherever there is love there is one who loves, one who is loved, and the love that exists between them). The twentieth-century theologian Karl Barth, following the passage through to its end, found the image of God in humanity as male and female. The image of God, Barth suggested, was as much between people as within them.

The Relationships of the Trinity

FATHER

The Father is
eternally Father of the Son.

SON

The Son is
eternally Son of the Father.

SPIRIT

The Spirit proceeds eternally
from the Father and the Son.

The Father loves the Son.
The Son loves the Father.
The Father loves the Spirit.
The Spirit loves the Father.
The Son loves the Spirit.
The Spirit loves the Son.

Humans also cannot be defined simply by attributes—"thinking beings" or "featherless bipeds." They must be defined by relationships. The self is not a simple thing. It is a whole web of relationships, and there are further relationships between selves. My mind, my heart (understood as a symbol of all the human emotions), and my body are all in a relationship with each other. I as a person am in relationship with numerous others. I cannot be a spouse, a parent, a friend, a colleague, or a teacher unless I have a spouse, children, friends, colleagues, and students. You cannot understand me, and I cannot understand myself, without taking some account of all these relationships.

Finally, you and I and all people everywhere are in relationship with the relational God. God is our creator, our redeemer, our desire, our goal. God is our friend, our brother or sister, our judge, our substitute. God is everywhere all the time, yet we long for God as if God were absent from us. The same Augustine of Hippo who wrote on the Trinity began his spiritual autobiography, *Confessions*, with these often-quoted words: "Thou hast made us for thyself and restless is our heart until it comes to rest in thee."[5] Our restless hearts are seeking God, although we might not always know that it is God we are seeking. If we are beings of relationship, and supremely beings of relationship with God, we cannot find ourselves, know ourselves, or be at peace with ourselves without finding God. This is the "other" we seek, the relationship that is the most important aspect of our lives.

SPIRITUALITY

Jesus called this the greatest commandment: "You shall love the Lord your God with all your heart, and with all your soul, and with all your might" (Deut. 6:5). This brings us face-to-face with another paradox: This commandment commands that which cannot be commanded. We humans cannot love on command. Loving is not like walking across the floor or mowing the lawn. Those sorts of things we can do when others order us to do them. We might grumble or protest or deliberately do a terrible job, but we can be forced to do them—and do them over if need be.

Love is not like that. Any attempt to coerce love, to squeeze it out of us, is only going to kill love all the more quickly. We only love when we meet that which is lovely and lovable. We love as a *response*. We might be responding to beauty, or friendliness, or some inner urge, or love itself. The point is, we are responding. To love God, then, we must know God as lovable and lovely. We must know God as love.

Spirituality is our fulfilling the commandment of Deuteronomy 6:5. Spirituality is our coming to understand God as lovely, lovable, and love itself.

There are techniques and disciplines in spirituality. There are important books. There are, or may be, spiritual guides and spiritual friends. Following the techniques, observing the disciplines, reading the books, attending to the guides, and being in communion with the spiritual friends are important parts of the spiritual life. But they all are means rather than ends or goals. To confuse them with spirituality itself is like thinking we have arrived in Cleveland just because we're standing on an asphalt highway.

The difference between God and Cleveland (or at least one of them) is that Cleveland isn't going to make any attempt to come to us. But God will.

SEPARATION AND SIN

Relationship implies difference. I can be related to people and things because they are somehow different from me. My children are not me. My spouse is not me. My teachers, my colleagues, and my students are not me.

I can be related to God because God is not me and I am not God. There is a distance, a separation between God and me. God created me, and I am God's creature. God is eternal, and I am bound by time. God is omnipotent, and I am weak. God is all-knowing, and I live in a sea of ignorance and error.

This separation is good and right. But there is another separation between God and humans that is not good and right. This separation is occasioned by human sin. Most of us have a rather adolescent understanding of sin as that which is forbidden by our parents, our churches, or our society—and presumably by God. Why? Mostly, we think, because it's too much fun or it feels too good. Sin in this sense is what you can't do until you come of age and live on your own.

This is not sin. It might involve "sins," or it might simply be social convention. Sin is deeper and deadlier than that.

Many of the documents in the *Book of Confessions* contain definitions of sin. This passage, from the Second Helvetic Confession, is typical: "By sin we understand that innate corruption of man which has been derived or propagated in us all from our first parents, by which we, immersed in perverse desires and averse to all good, are inclined to all evil" (*BC* 5.037). This sounds odd to contemporary ears. It seems both harsh and quaint, and evokes images of witch trials and stocks on the village green. Are we really "immersed in perverse desires and averse to all good?" Why doesn't the *Book of Confessions* acknowledge that many of us are genuinely trying to lead good lives? It is the little word *trying* that gives the game away. The fact that we have to try so hard to lead good lives is an indication that there is something deep within us that is resisting our effort to live rightly and is enticing us to something quite different.

Sins are deeds—deeds of violence, deeds of self-centeredness, deeds of indifference to the condition of others. Sin is the condition of separation from and opposition to God that gives rise to such deeds. God's otherness, God's distance from us, is not just the distance between the Creator and the created. It is the difference between holiness and corruption, selfless love and self-obsession. The pain of our separation from God is, in part, the pain of our separation from what we were created to be. Humans were not created evil, but they have succumbed to it. Bad things are done by good people, even the best people. Life for even the best people is a struggle to choose what is good over what is not. And the best people are rare. Some around us seem to have simply given themselves to evil. Most of us do not want that, either for ourselves or for our world. Yet Paul's words seem to describe our lives: "I do not understand my own actions. For I do not do what I want, but I do the very thing I hate" (Rom. 7:15).

The situation is not hopeless. Indeed, it is profoundly hopeful. This is the content of the gospel message: God has accomplished that which was beyond our power. This pervasive pull of sin is universal—everyone feels it, everyone knows it, everyone contends with it—but it is not invincible. At least, not for God. That changes everything. God's coming to us involves God's over-coming of not just our deeds but our condition. Sins and sin are vanquished. There is healing, and there is hope. The convalescence, however, might be protracted and arduous.

CHURCH

In its primary and most important sense, the church is people. Secondarily, the church is the building in which those people regularly gather.

The church might be a beloved people and a treasured place for you. It might be a place of profound alienation that you avoid as much as you can. It might be a place where you have been valued and treasured. It might be a place where you were abused and deeply wounded. Or you might have had no direct experience with church at all. The most common charge made against the church is that it is not what it could or should be. It is not what it claims to be or is called to be. It is a group of people who are profoundly and shock-ingly hypocritical.

All this is true. In fact, in the Reformed tradition it is an article of faith that the church is made up of sinners and is itself sinful. But the sinfulness of the church does not nullify the power of God to work in and through the church. The Westminster Confession is characteristically blunt on this point: "The purest churches under heaven are subject to both mixture [of the pure and not so pure] and error; and some have so degenerated as to become apparently no churches of Christ. Nevertheless, there shall be always a Church on earth, to worship God according to his will" (BC 6.144).[6]

The church persists in spite of its own sin because of the power of God. In these times, it is being called to become an oasis for seekers as well as a home for believers. This is a change in some respects; in others, it is no change at all. Instead, it is a renewal, for the church's true mission has never been sheer self-perpetuation or increase for the sake of increase.

The Confession of 1967 particularly emphasizes this point. The church has a mission, and its mission is its life: "To be reconciled to God is to be sent into the world as his reconciling community. This community, the church universal, is entrusted with God's message of reconciliation and shares his labor of healing the enmities which separate men from God and from each other" (BC 9.31). This is the task not just of the church as such, but of each individual within the church. A true spirituality enables this mission, for it fosters the healing of relationships within the individual, between individuals, and between humanity and God. A spirituality that divides and isolates the individual, thereby producing an attitude of indifference to the world and the world's peoples, is a betrayal of the church's mission and therefore of the gospel itself.

In a sense, the church is like a hospital. Everyone within is recovering from the wounding of the spirit that comes about through the sin in the world and within oneself. No one is entirely well, and some seem to be getting worse. Nevertheless, it is a hospital and not a mortuary. One can look around any church and see the sin, the hypocrisy, the lassitude. But one can also see people getting better. This ability to see people getting better might be a sign that one is getting better oneself.

TRADITIONS, REFORMED AND OTHERWISE

A tradition is a way of being a Christian that has evolved through time. Traditions involve shared history, shared beliefs, shared styles of worship, and a shared ethos. We receive traditions through teaching and example. We live them and possibly transform them in the living. We hand them on to those who follow us.

Christianity itself has been termed a tradition. Within Christianity, one can point to several traditions: Eastern Orthodox, Roman Catholic, Episcopal, Lutheran, Reformed, free church, and so on. At one time, the traditions tended to view each other with hostility, some of which is quite apparent in certain of the documents in the *Book of Confessions*. The ecumenical movement of the last several decades, combined with the effects of the Second Vatican Council, has done a great deal to lessen some of the hostility. Whereas once many traditions claimed that they were the only way of being Christian, now they (or at least most of them) are more likely to claim validity rather than exclusivity—"Our tradition is a way of being a Christian, but it is not necessarily the *only* way of being a Christian."

This is explicitly stated in the Confession of 1967: "The institutions of the people of God change and vary as their mission requires in different times and places. The unity of the church is compatible with a wide variety of forms, but it is hidden and distorted when variant forms are allowed to harden into sectarian divisions, exclusive denominations, and rival factions" (*BC* 9.34). One can find the influence of the ecumenical movement throughout the Confession of 1967 not only in its content and presentation but in the very fact that it created a *Book of Confessions* consisting of documents from the entire history (including the pre-Reformation history) of the church, instead of simply relying on the Westminster Standards.

This change in attitude has made it easier to borrow from other traditions. This is especially true in the area of spirituality. The increasing interest in spirituality over the last several decades can be traced largely to the worldwide influence of Thomas Merton, a Roman Catholic monk. Christians of all traditions read Merton, and still do so, with great profit. Merton himself, after spending years immersed in the writings of St. Teresa of Avila and St. John of the Cross, began reading Protestant theologians, notably Karl Barth and Dietrich Bonhoeffer, at about the same time he was devouring works by Zen masters and Sufi mystics. This eclecticism has shaped contemporary spirituality.

This does not mean that traditions have become archaic or unimportant. On the contrary, they are now more important than ever. In some ways, a tradition is like a part in a play. A play has a script, which contains a description of a character, the words the character is supposed to say, and the actions the character is supposed to carry out. This might seem restrictive and confining, but it is not. Actors must interpret the parts, and no two actors play a part exactly the same way. Similarly, Christians receive their tradition and embody it with their lives. No two Christians have embodied a tradition exactly the same way. They have embodied the traditions according to their imaginations, intelligences, and individual circumstances. Living according to a tradition both demands and engenders extraordinary creativity and resourcefulness.

The Reformed tradition traces itself to sixteenth-century Switzerland, particularly to two cities and two individuals: Ulrich Zwingli in Zurich and John Calvin in Geneva. *Calvinism* has come to be almost synonymous with *Reformed tradition*. This testifies to the extraordinary influence Calvin had in shaping the tradition, but he was not the founder or initiator of the movement in the sense that Luther was the founder of Lutheranism. Many other figures helped embody and transform the tradition: John Knox in Scotland, Zacharias Ursinus and Kaspar Oleviamus in Heidelberg (the authors of the Heidelberg Catechism), Heinrich Bullinger in Zurich (the author of the Second Helvetic Confession, as well as a First Helvetic Confession that is not included in the *Book of Confessions*), and Jonathan Edwards in America. Recently, Karl Barth has influenced theology everywhere, and his multivolume *Church Dogmatics* stands among the most significant theological writings in the entire history of the Christian faith.

What does it mean to live according to the Reformed tradition? It does not mean that you should conduct yourself as if you were a resident of sixteenth-century Switzerland or eighteenth-century New England. It does mean that you are willing to be instructed by the people who lived in those times. It also means that you will consider crucial what they considered crucial—"the affirmation of the majesty, holiness, and providence of God who creates, sustains, rules, and redeems the world in the freedom of sovereign righteousness and love," as the *Book of Order* puts it (F-2.05). This affirmation is not just verbal. It is not simply a matter of saying, "Yes, I believe in this God." It is a matter of living, of submitting to this God in humility and responding to the love of this God with your life. It is, in fact, loving the Lord your God with all your heart, and with all your soul, and with all your might over the days and weeks and months and years of your life.

How does one do that? That is what the rest of this book is about.

QUESTIONS FOR COMPREHENSION AND SELF-EXPLORATION

1. What does it mean to say that language about God is "analogical?"
2. How do you think of God? In pictures? Single words? Stories?
3. What description, image, or symbol of God is most important to you? Why? What descriptions, images, or symbols of God do you reject? Why?

2

Some Questions

The Spiritual Life Today

A painting hangs in the Boston Museum of Fine Art whose title asks three questions: *Where Do We Come From? What Are We? Where Are We Going?* The painting itself, a triptych of scenes set in Tahiti, is on one level perfectly ordinary. In the first scene, some women are gathered around a baby. In the second, a young man is picking some fruit. In the final scene, an old woman sits with her head in her hands. Symbolically, this painting presents the mystery of human life. It does not answer the three questions of the title; it merely poses them.

These questions are universal. There is scarcely a human alive who has not asked them in one way or another. The answers, however, seem to be elusive.

Most of the world's religions provide answers to these questions, and Christianity is no exception. The Christian answers are these: "We come from God. We are God's children. We are returning to God." These answers do not dispel the mystery, but they do locate it. The mystery has to do with God and our relationship to God.

Our coming from God is out of our hands. We have no say in when and how and where and to whom we come. Our returning to God is also out of our hands, with one caveat. We cannot choose whether we will die, and for the most part we cannot choose how we will die.

Between the coming from God and the returning to God, however, there is much that is in our own hands, at least partially. We make real decisions, we choose between whatever alternatives are open to us, and we can try to do this in responsible ways. We are held accountable for the choices we make, both by ourselves and by our society. To this extent, we are free. It is a general principle that if one is not free, one cannot be held responsible for one's actions.

We grow into that freedom. The process of maturation is in large part learning how to make the best use of our freedom. We do not allow infants much freedom at all, for they do not yet have the ability to make choices and carry them out. Children gradually gain this freedom, but it takes a while—two or three decades, and sometimes more. As we mature, we require less external guidance because as we gain intelligence and experience, we become more and more capable of guiding ourselves. Gaining freedom is thus not simply a lessening of restraint. It is a growing internal discipline replacing external restraint. If this growing internal discipline is lacking, people become dangerous—a threat to themselves and others.

ON HUMAN DEVELOPMENT

While everyone's path to maturity is different, all such paths have some features in common. Over the past several decades, behavioral scientists from many disciplines have been charting human development, attempting to correlate how physical, psychological, and social growth interact. Jean Piaget investigated cognitive growth in children, Eric Kohlberg examined the stages of moral growth, and James Fowler delineated stages of religious development. In his notable work *Childhood and Society*, Erik Erikson proposed a comprehensive mapping of human development, in which maturation depends on the successful resolution of the basic conflicts people experience as they grow.[1] These conflicts span the entire course of human life. They demonstrate that development occurs throughout one's life. People face different sorts of tasks at different stages of life. While Erikson's work does not deal directly with issues of spiritual development, the resolution (or lack thereof) of these conflicts is deeply related to one's spiritual growth.

The work of the psychiatrist Carl Jung has been particularly influential in modern spirituality. Jung's concept of human life maintains that every person has two fundamental tasks: the discovery of one's place in the world and the exploration of one's true self.[2] The discovery of one's place in the world is the work of the first half of life. It involves acquiring knowledge and skills, choosing a career, establishing a home of one's own, finding a life partner, and bearing and raising children. At the heart of this is the ability to separate oneself from one's parents (psychically if not physically) in order to establish one's own identity.[3]

Jung understands the discovery of one's true self to be the work of the second half of life. This work involves the rejection of (or at least the recognition of) social roles, the recognition of one's "shadow," the integration of one's conscious and unconscious minds, and the union with a "higher" self, which Jung at one point calls, "God within us."[4] What Jung means by "God" is a matter of some dispute, and more than a little confusion. One need not, however, adopt Jung's conception of God in order to be illuminated by his analysis of the fundamental tasks of human life. The questions "What is my place in the world?" and "Who am I really?" are asked by everyone and are answered only by the living of life itself.

These two questions can be understood spiritually only in terms of relationships. "What is my place in the world?" has to do with education, employment, geographic locale, family, friends, sexual orientation, social class, and a host of other factors. Spiritually, however, has to do with God—or more particularly, with God's call to each individual to share in God's work. In theological terms, *vocation* is not restricted to one's training or employment. It is one's sharing in the tasks of building the kingdom of God.

The Confession of 1967 states, "Life is a gift to be received with gratitude and a task to be pursued with courage" (*BC* 9.17). The task is sometimes a "Go here and do this" command, along the lines of a military order. More often, though, it is a challenge that requires discernment, improvisation, freedom, love, and intelligence: "The Church disperses to serve God wherever its members are, at work or play, in private or in the life of society. . . . Their daily action in the world is the church in mission to the world" (*BC* 9.37). The Reformed tradition has consistently refused either to be enslaved by the world or to abandon it.

"Who am I really?" would seem to be a question about one's individual identity or inner being. But it also is about relationship—one's relationship with God. As we saw in the last chapter, our relationship with God makes us who we are, and to seek our true self is to seek God, although perhaps not under that name.

These two questions lead to the two movements of the spiritual life. People have described these movements in different ways. In their book *The Spiritual Journey: Critical Thresholds and Stages of Adult Spiritual Genesis*, Francis Kelly Nemeck and Marie Theresa Coombs term them "immersion in creation" and "emergence through creation."[5] More simply, Betsy Caprio and Thomas Hedberg call them "leaving home" and "coming home."[6] The basic principle, however described, is this: All things come from God, and all things return to God. This is true of the cosmos itself; its going forth from God is called creation, and its returning to God is termed redemption or consummation. Christ's going forth from God is called *kenosis*, after the Greek word used in Philippians 2:7, translated as "emptied" in the New Revised Standard Version. His return to God is his exaltation. Our own going forth from God is our birth; our return is our death.

We see the same pattern in many of the biblical narratives. Jacob goes forth—or rather, runs away—from the land of his fathers and then ultimately returns to it. The people of Israel go into Egypt and are led back to the promised land by Moses and Joshua. Much later, the people of Judah are taken to Babylon as slaves, ultimately to return when Babylon is conquered by Persia. In the New Testament, Jesus sends the disciples out, and they return to him (Mark 6:7–13; Luke 10:1–20).

Finally, the pattern is repeated liturgically each week. The church begins the week by gathering for worship and fellowship. The congregation disperses during the week, as people live out their lives in human cultures. As the Confession of 1967 puts it, "Wherever the church exists, its members are both gathered in corporate life and dispersed in society for the sake of mission to the world" (*BC* 9.35).

This pattern of going out and returning, then, is constantly repeated—in our lives, in our history, and in our cosmos. This pattern not only forms the context for our questions but also determines the way the questions will be answered. We cannot determine our place in the world abstractly; we can only make some guesses about what it might be. To find the actual place, we must go forth into the world—to explore, to experiment, to try, to risk, even to fail. We cannot discover our real self without learning that simply knowing our place in the world is not enough. We must have some sense of who we are regardless of our place in the world or our personal circumstances at any given point in our lives. Our return is a matter of discovering or revitalizing the eternal relationship with God that makes us who we are.

THE FIRST QUESTION:
WHAT IS MY PLACE IN THE WORLD?

Are the two questions "What is my place in the world?" and "Who am I, really?" answered sequentially or simultaneously? Jung suggests that the second question cannot be addressed until the first one is somehow settled. Since the discovery of the true self depends on the transcendence or destruction of the social self, the true self must wait until there is a social self to destroy.[7]

No matter when the questions are answered, however, both are asked early and often. They differ according to how much power each question has at different stages of life. It tends to be the case that the question "What is my place in the world?" is the more powerful one in the first half of life. Any number of factors enter into one's "place": Who is my family? Who are my friends? What is my religious community—or do I even have a religious community? What is my school? What careers am I interested in? What is my sexual orientation? Whom will I marry, or will I marry at all? Do I want to have children?

There is a kind of anguish involved in the search for one's place, especially if one begins to suspect that one has no place at all. The adolescent "loner," however much he or she projects an I-don't-care cynical bravado, is a person in pain. Even though most teenagers ultimately do manage to find a way to make peace with the world, or at least find an endurable compromise, the trauma of feeling uncoordinated, unpopular, unsuccessful, or unloved lasts for years. The deeper wounds of molestation or physical and sexual abuse can affect a person for a lifetime.

Nemeck and Coombs rightly suggest that the process of finding one's place often proceeds through exclusion: by exploring and rejecting various options, one finds the places where one does fit.[8] This is accompanied by considerable anxiety, for it involves exploring the unfamiliar and risking the unknown. Religiously, such an exploration might involve visiting different denominations or even different religious traditions before finding a community in which one feels at home. It might mean rejecting religion altogether—or for those who come from families with no religious affiliation or activity, a wholehearted embrace of any and all things characterized as religious. Even if one never seeks an alternative to one's own religious upbringing, there comes a moment when a person must accept that upbringing as one's own and appropriate it for oneself, rather than passively accepting that which one has inherited.

This appropriation does not necessarily take the form of a "conversion experience," although it certainly might. Neither is it simply intellectual assent to doctrinal propositions. In essence, it is the resolve to live in a certain way, based on certain convictions one holds to be true. These convictions come from the teaching of the community; in that sense, they come from outside oneself. But they also are one's own, in the sense that they express one's belief, trust, and commitment.

The issue of experience versus doctrinal assent has been a very troubling one for American Christianity. The series of Great Awakenings that began in the 1730s and that led to the phenomenon of revivalism affected almost every denomination in America. In some cases, it led to deep divisions and even separations, which were overcome only with enormous difficulty.

The *Book of Confessions* does not demand or presuppose any particular kind of spiritual or emotional experience as a prerequisite for church membership. It does demand a sacramental experience: the experience of baptism. Baptism is seen as a declaration of the grace of God in symbolic form with respect to a particular individual. That which is symbolized, in the words of the Confession of 1967, is "not only cleansing from sin, but a dying with Christ and a joyful rising with him to new life" (*BC* 9.51). Objectively, the cleansing, dying, and rising are simply a fact: This is how the individual is with God. It is the result of the work of Christ. Subjectively, the effects of this are lifelong: "The efficacy of Baptism is not tied to that moment of time wherein it is administered; yet, notwithstanding, by the right use of this ordinance the grace promised is not only offered, but really exhibited and conferred by the Holy Ghost" (*BC* 6.159).

The resolution of the question "What is my place in the world?" on a spiritual level is more than finding a congenial religious community. It is finding a spiritual *calling*—a vocation. It is finding some task—which might or might not be the way one earns a living—that expresses and enacts one's faith. For some, this might involve definite religious professions: the pastoral ministry, a monastic community, mission work. Others might choose professions that embody religious values—healing or helping professions, teaching, counseling. Others might simply do their work as well as they can, trusting that in so doing they are glorifying God. Some will work out their religious commitments through voluntary activities. There are many ways to do the Lord's work, surely as many as there are people to do it.

THE SECOND QUESTION: WHO AM I REALLY?

In some sense, the discovery of one's place in the world is also a discovery of self. It might even be regarded as a construction of self, in that one's social self is always in some sense a construct. Sooner or later, though, people will begin to ask, "Who am I, no matter *where* I am? Who is the real me?" It tends to become the pressing question in the later part of life, especially when people begin to feel the distance between what they do and who they think they are (or might be). Especially if people start to feel that there might not be a "real me," that they have become replaceable parts in a mass society that exploits and manipulates its members rather than enhancing and honoring them, the search for one's authentic self becomes a matter of survival.

The last half of life is marked by a number of "passivities of diminishment," to use Nemeck and Coombs's phrase—diminishment because we experience losses around us and within us, and passivities because we can do little or nothing to arrest these losses.[9] We will inevitably age. We will inevitably lose physical capacity. We will likely become increasingly dependent on others. Finally, we will die. Our friends and family members, who are also aging, will go through the same process.

It is possible, of course, to ignore all this. It is possible to deny it. It is possible, and not at all unusual, to spend enormous amounts of money trying to recapture (or reenact) one's youth. It is possible, but it is not helpful in the quest for one's true self and unique value. The first essential of that quest is honest acknowledgment of the pain and grief of these unavoidable diminishments. They are not disasters. They are, in fact, necessary stages on the way of return.

How does one go about answering the question "Who am I, really?" First, one must turn around. In whatever far country one finds oneself, one must ask, "What is the way home?" In the parable of the Prodigal Son, the son's return home begins when he recovers his sense of who he is: "But when he came to himself he said, 'How many of my father's hired hands have bread enough and to spare, but here I am dying of hunger! I will get up and go to my father'" (Luke 15:17–18a). The son's way home is not simply a return to a place; it is a return to a relationship. The son recognizes that his behavior might have altered the relationship, and he is willing to accept that: "I will say to him, 'Father, I have sinned against heaven and before you; I am no longer worthy to be called your son; treat me like one of your hired hands'" (Luke 15:18b–19). Nothing in the parable describes the actual journey home, but one cannot imagine that it would have been easy.

Not every going forth is an exercise in prodigality, of course. If the aim of the going forth is to find one's role in the unfolding kingdom of God, it is an exercise in obedience. But every coming home must involve some element of coming to oneself—and to come to oneself is to come to a restoration or renewal of that which is in relationship with oneself.

THE WAY HOME: THE MOVEMENTS OF LATER LIFE

The transitions involved in the second half of life are variable and often painful, but they can also be fruitful. Following are descriptions of some of the movements involved in the process of returning home.

The Acceptance of Finitude

Finitude is one of the givens of human life. Our power is limited, our knowledge is limited, our life span is limited. Even at our most potent we can be hurt, and we are seldom at our most potent. As the years pass, we lose mental and physical capacity, and we are increasingly subject to injury and illness. We will age, and we will die.

When we are young, all this seems rather abstract. As we get older, it becomes not only *a* reality, but *our* reality. We can deny it, or we can fight it. We can act as if we are young, even when we are no longer young, or we can accept our aging and its consequences, both for the pain and the gifts it brings.

This acceptance in part lies in keeping ourselves as healthy and fit as we can. This is not in order to recapture a lost youth, but to make the most of our present. In part, however, acceptance involves the recognition that passivities of diminishment will occur, including the ultimate passivity—our death. In

that death, we lose the last shred of our ability to act or alter our circumstances. We lie entirely in God's hands. Approaching death, we must remember that those hands are strong hands, and they have been around us all along.

The Recognition of Sinfulness

Finitude as such is not sinful. Finitude is an attribute of ourselves as creatures—beings created by God. Sin is our rebellion against God.

The *Book of Confessions* tends to associate human sinfulness with the story of
the fall in Genesis 2–3. This passage from the Second Helvetic Confession is
typical: "By sin we understand that innate corruption of man which has been
derived or propagated in us all from our first parents, by which we, immersed
in perverse desires and averse to all good, are inclined to all evil. Full of all
wickedness, distrust, contempt and hatred of God, we are unable to do or
even to think anything good of ourselves" (*BC* 5.037). The universality of sin,
however, is not tied to a literal understanding of this passage. The Confession of 1967 considers human sinfulness in the light of the revelation of Jesus
Christ: "Wise and virtuous men through the ages have sought the highest
good in devotion to freedom, justice, peace, truth, and beauty. Yet all human
virtue, when seen in the light of God's love in Jesus Christ, is found to be
infected by self-interest and hostility. All men, good and bad alike, are in the
wrong before God and helpless without his forgiveness" (*BC* 9.13). Human
sinfulness is a revealed truth, revealed only in the light of the grace of God.
The knowledge that we are sinners does not precede the knowledge that we
are forgiven sinners; it follows from that knowledge.

The Reformed tradition has always sought to be honest about human sinfulness. The risk it has run is to be obsessed with human sinfulness, as if that
sinfulness were the primary reality in our relationship with God. But if all the
gospel had to tell us is that we are sinful, it would scarcely be good news, or
news at all. Instead, the gospel is the declaration of God's grace in the face
of human sin. It is the triumph of grace over sin. The reality of sin does not
jeopardize or obliterate the power of God's grace.

Recognizing our sinfulness is more than acknowledging the general sinfulness of humanity. It is acknowledging our own particular sins, our own
particular temptations, and our own particular rebellions. Furthermore, it is
realizing that not all of our sinning is behind us. As long as we are alive on
this earth, we will be sinners in need of God's grace, sinners in spite of our
best intentions and strongest effort. Paul's words in Romans describe every
Christian: "I do not understand my own actions. For I do not do what I want,
but I do the very thing I hate" (Rom. 7:15).

This does not mean that we are entitled or expected to sin with abandon. The universality of sin and our recognition of our own sin do not constitute permission to sin. Neither does it entitle us to simply despair and give up the effort to lead a life acceptable to God. Rather, it asks us to honestly and sincerely attempt to live such a life, and to trust that God's grace will always be with us in that attempt.

This process is made explicit in the Westminster Confession:

> Men ought not to content themselves with a general repentance, but it is every man's duty to repent of his particular sins, particularly. As every man is bound to make private confession of his sins to God, praying for the pardon thereof, upon which, and the forsaking of them, he shall find mercy: so he that scandalizeth his brother, or the church of Christ, ought to be willing, by a private or public confession and sorrow for his sin, to declare his repentance to those who are offended; who are thereupon to be reconciled to him, and in love to receive him. (*BC* 6.085–6.086)

It is generally recognized that honest acknowledgment of one's particular sins is necessary for the healing of mind, heart, and soul. The Reformed tradition holds that such acknowledgment is not the precondition or presupposition for grace, but the consequence of it. Without the prior assistance of God's grace, the recognition and amendment of our sin is impossible. Consequently, it is impossible to recognize oneself as a sinner apart from God's grace: To know oneself as a sinner, one knows oneself as a forgiven sinner. Regret might come unaccompanied, but repentance can only occur when one learns to trust in God's grace.

The Movement toward Trust

Trust is fundamental to human life, whatever one's age. Erikson lists trust versus mistrust as the very first conflict of development, characteristic of infancy. Is the world a trustworthy place or not? Will those who care for me respond to my needs or not? Infants who experience the world as untrustworthy or their caregivers as unreliable or dangerous can sustain lifelong damage. One of the basic tasks of parents, or all who care for infants, is to give the kind of care and attention that will establish this trust.

Trust in God is related to, but not identical with, experiencing the world as trustworthy. The world is a very ambiguous place, and the biblical view of the world reflects this. On the one hand, the world—the created order—is unequivocally good. The first chapter of the book of Genesis is not only an account of creation but also an extended benediction on creation. Each thing that is created is pronounced good, and the entire creation, all that God made, is pronounced "very good" (Gen. 1:31). But the world also is Satan's arena, and he is often termed "the ruler of this world."

Faith in God, according to the *Book of Confessions*, is not simply the belief that there is a God. Faith, rather, is trust in God. The first question of the Heidelberg Catechism demonstrates this:

> Q. 1. What is your only comfort, in life and in death?

> A. That I belong—body and soul, in life and in death—not to myself but to my faithful Savior, Jesus Christ, who at the cost of his own blood has fully paid for all my sins and has completely freed me from the dominion of the devil; that he protects me so well that without the will of my Father in heaven not a hair can fall from my head; indeed, that everything must fit his purpose for my salvation. Therefore, by his Holy Spirit, he also assures me of eternal life, and makes me wholeheartedly willing and ready from now on to live for him. (*BC* 4.001)

Trust in God, according to this passage, is based on what God has done already, and not just on what God will do. It certainly is not the belief that nothing unpleasant or painful will happen in the future. Rather, it is the awareness that God is present and active always, no matter what is happening in the world or in one's personal life.

The strength of one's trust is often a day-to-day thing. It is a great mistake to judge the strength of one's faith by the depth of one's feeling. Sometimes belief is strong; sometimes it is elusive. Crisis often brings doubts. Nevertheless, trust in God can grow as people mature. They can develop the capacity to say to themselves, "As it has been, so it shall be." Paul writes, "For I am convinced that neither death, nor life, nor angels, nor rulers, nor things present, nor things to come, nor powers, nor height, nor depth, nor anything else in all creation, will be able to separate us from the love of God in Christ Jesus our Lord" (Rom. 8:38–39). These words do not deny the reality of hard and painful things in life. They simply say that nothing can overcome or drive away God's love.

The Movement toward Contemplation

The movement from action to contemplation is often a characteristic of a maturing faith. *Contemplation* is a fundamental, albeit rather controversial, word in the history of Christian spirituality. It is often used to describe a kind of life that is held to be superior to life in the world. Mary and Martha (Luke 10:38–42) are allegorized into two types of life (withdrawn from the world or active within the world) or two states (praying or working), and one is held to be superior to the other.

The Reformed tradition, and Protestantism in general, has been suspicious of such a division of life. It has generally held that the proper task of the Christian is to transform life, rather than endure it or withdraw from it.

The polemic against monasticism characteristic of the *Book of Confessions* documents from the sixteenth and seventeenth centuries gives a rather sharp tone to the passages concerning the duties of a Christian. In the Westminster Confession, for example, we read, "Monastical vows of perpetual single life, professed poverty, and regular obedience, are so far from being degrees of higher perfection, that they are superstitious and sinful snares, in which no Christian may entangle himself" (*BC* 6.126). This hostility toward monasticism has dissipated over the last several decades, in part because of the influence of monks such as Thomas Merton, who found an enormous audience of Protestants and Catholics, and in part because of Protestant experiments in monasticism, notably the Iona Community in Scotland and the Taizé Community in France.

The word *contemplation* does not have to refer to anything other than resting quietly in the presence of God. It can involve a wordless prayer, an interior quiet, or simply an awareness of the divine in our midst. The realization that prayer does not have to involve words, intentions, or emotions but can simply be resting in openness to God's presence often shapes people's spiritual practices in the second half of life.

The Westminster Shorter Catechism begins with this question and answer:

Q. 1. What is the chief end of man?

A. Man's chief end is to glorify God, and to enjoy him forever." (*BC* 7.001)

The word *enjoy*, which is often slighted, means much more than "takes pleasure in." We do not enjoy God the way we might enjoy a piece of cake or a good movie. Rather, *enjoy* means both "to experience" and "to gain joy from." In other words, we humans are intended to rejoice in God's presence forever. No distinction is made here between earthly life and whatever lies beyond earthly life. Enjoying God forever is not only what awaits us; it is what can and should be here and now. The Reformed tradition is often depicted as maintaining that the service of God is a burdensome and dreary thing. The confessions teach quite the opposite: the service of God—the glorification of God through obedience to the Word of God—is full of joy. Contemplation in this context is precisely enjoying God: here, now, and forever.

The Movement toward Serenity

Serenity is the emotional response that accompanies acceptance of one's fini-tude and sinfulness. Serenity in this sense is more than impassivity, equanim-ity, or stoicism. It does not come from within a person. Rather, it comes from the growing relationship of love and trust between oneself and one's God. As Martin Luther's most famous hymn, "A Mighty Fortress Is Our God," puts it, "Did we in our own strength confide, our striving would be losing / Were not the right man on our side, the man of God's own choosing."

The passivities of diminishment in the last half of life are the cause of much frustration, sorrow, and grief. They teach hard lessons. One of the hardest is this separation of self from serenity. Our culture has stressed (in theory at least) independence, self-reliance, and the sense that asking for help or relying on others is shameful. Older people often say that their great-est fear is having to be dependent on someone else. This way of thinking is directly opposite to what the gospel teaches. It is not at all a shameful thing to rely on others. It is a part of the mutuality of Christians. "Bear one another's burdens," Paul writes, "and in this way you will fulfill the law of Christ" (Gal. 6:2).

We are, however, not strong enough to bear one another's burdens unless someone else is helping to bear ours. Collectively, as families or as congrega-tions, we are not strong enough to bear each other's burdens unless we are relying on God's strength instead of our own. Belief in God, if it transcends having an opinion that there is a something called "God," always has this character—and consequently, it leads toward serenity.

Again, the Heidelberg Catechism expresses this serenity and its basis:

> Q. 26. What do you believe when you say: "I believe in God the Father Almighty, Maker of heaven and earth?
>
> A. That the eternal Father of our Lord Jesus Christ, who out of noth-ing created heaven and earth with all that is in them, who also upholds and governs them by his eternal counsel and providence, is for the sake of Christ his Son my God and my Father. I trust in him so com-pletely that I have no doubt that he will provide me with all things necessary for body and soul. (BC 4.026)

Serenity in this sense is doubtless just as variable as trust. Some days we can accept disappointments and even disasters with equanimity. Other times, even slight setbacks can provoke anxiety and despair. Our emotional state at any given time is not an indication either of the constancy of God or of our own spiritual maturity. We see too little, know too little, and understand too imperfectly to attach any great importance to the moods of the moment.

A serene and trusting faith springs from knowing that God is trustworthy. The discovery of our true self lies in God. Introspection or self-analysis might be very helpful in many ways, but they are not enough. They lead us inward, to the interior self, when our going home lies outward, in the journey of the relational self. Again, we have a paradox: the true self becomes known through self-abandonment, not self-obsession. Serenity, trust, interior peace, going home, learning who we are, all happen on the way.

In the following chapters, we will explore this journey in some detail, first by considering stages of faith, then by considering stages of love. We will see the self in relation to God come clearer as we follow the dialectic of self-discovery through self-abandonment. First, however, we will take a closer look at the Reformed tradition itself and how it guides one in the spiritual life.

QUESTIONS FOR COMPREHENSION AND SELF-EXPLORATION

1. Describe how you found where you fit in your life. What were your key moments of discovery? When did you experience ambiguity or confusion?
2. What are your unique, valuable, or special characteristics?

3

Some Help

Tradition and the Spiritual Life

"Because of our traditions," says Tevye in the opening scene of *Fiddler on the Roof*, "every one of us knows who he is and what God expects him to do." That is not a simple thing, as the musical itself (and the Sholom Aleichem stories behind it) demonstrate. The knowledge that traditions give about who one is and what God expects one to do is not simple knowledge. It can be liberating and integrating, or it can be constricting and dehumanizing. How to make proper and appropriate use of tradition is one of the arts involved in living a human life. These two functions of tradition, to know who one is and what God expects one to do, correspond exactly to the two questions we discussed in the previous chapter: "What is my place in the world?" and "Who am I really?"

TRADITION AND RELIGION

Traditions are ways of doing things or ways of thinking that are handed on from person to person and generation to generation.[1] They are not necessarily religious; they can be simple customs or patterns of behavior: "It is our family tradition to have duck instead of turkey for Thanksgiving dinner." It can be said, however, that all religions *have* traditions, or at least develop them, and that that is one of the ways religions perpetuate themselves through time.

Traditions enable a religion to mediate between continuity and change. As religions encounter new challenges and circumstances, they must adapt and respond in ways that do not threaten their fundamental identity. This can often be a difficult struggle.

31

The early church endured many such struggles. Jesus' deeds and teachings were not simply passed on from person to person. They were applied by various communities to a number of situations, producing not one tradition but many. Contemporary biblical scholars devote much of their efforts to identifying and understanding these communities, their histories, and their needs.

Sometimes the teachings of various individuals or groups were judged to have compromised the faith rather than perpetuated it. These teachings, judged "heresies," were combated by various means: oral opposition, written refutation, promulgation of creeds, and finalization of the canon of writings that constituted sacred Scripture. Heresies were often the mother of orthodoxy, in the sense that they forced the church to define and articulate its beliefs in response to those who seemed to threaten or pervert it.

The Nicene Creed, for example, took an element of the liturgy of baptism and pressed it into service as a way of combating the heresy of Arianism, which questioned the divinity of the Son of God. The establishment of the canon of the New Testament (the determination of which works did and did not belong in the New Testament) was done in opposition to various groups who wanted either to expand or to reduce the list of sacred writings. Marcion, who lived in the second century, argued that the church's canon ought to be limited to certain of the Pauline epistles and the Gospel of Luke (as edited by Marcion himself). He excluded the entire Old Testament and a good bit of the New. Others argued that various Gospels (e.g., the Gospel of Peter, the Gospel of Thomas) or other writings ought to be included. The discussion over the contents of the canon lasted well into the fourth century.

THE CHRISTIAN TRADITION AND CHRISTIAN TRADITIONS

The term *Christian tradition*, in the words of the noted historian Jaroslav Pelikan, is "the form which . . . Christian doctrine has taken in history."[2] The term *tradition* is also often used to speak of various families within the Christian tradition. In the Evening Prayers of the *Book of Common Worship*, ten such families are named (and prayed for on successive nights): Roman Catholic; Orthodox and Coptic; Episcopal and Methodist; Baptist, Disciples of Christ, and other free churches; and Reformed, Presbyterian, and Lutheran.[3] This enumeration is intended to be reasonably comprehensive, so that in the course of a week the entire Christian church is lifted up in prayer, tradition by tradition.

Throughout their histories, the various traditions have spent a good deal of time and energy attacking, vilifying, excommunicating, and anathematizing each other. To the extent that each considered itself the one true church, it also considered the others false: perverted, heretical, dangerous, and some-times (all too often, in fact) the Antichrist. The so-called Great Schism, in which the Roman Catholic and Eastern Orthodox Churches excommuni-cated each other, occurred in 1054. During the Council of Trent (1545–1563), Roman Catholics condemned most forms of Protestantism, which had already castigated Roman Catholicism as morally corrupt and doctrinally apostate. Henry VIII of England broke from the Roman Catholic Church in 1534, which promptly excommunicated him. Certain of the documents con-tained in the *Book of Confessions* contain language about other traditions that many Presbyterians find shocking but that truly reflect the attitudes of the time in which they were written.

The worldwide ecumenical movement of the twentieth century along with developments in the Roman Catholic and Eastern Orthodox realms have resulted in a new spirit among the various traditions. The days of open war-fare and blanket condemnations seem nearly to be gone. Rather than claiming exclusivity, many of the traditions are maintaining *validity*: they represent a valid way of being Christian, but not the only possible way.

The "Foundations of Presbyterian Polity" section in the *Book of Order* expresses this concept of valid but not exclusive. On the one hand, "the creeds and confessions of this church arise in response to particular circumstances within the history of God's people. They claim the truth of the Gospel at those points where the authors perceived that truth to be at risk. They are the result of prayer, thought, and experience within a living tradition" (F-2.01). Never-theless, "division into different denominations obscures but does not destroy unity in Christ. The Presbyterian Church (U.S.A.), affirming its historical con-tinuity with the whole Church of Jesus Christ, is committed to the reduction of that obscurity and is willing to seek and to deepen communion with all other churches within the one, holy, catholic, and apostolic Church" (F-1.03a).

This openness to other Christian (and even non-Christian) traditions has been especially evident in the areas of worship and spirituality. The preface to the 1993 *Book of Common Worship* notes an "ecumenical convergence" in contemporary worship, based upon the need for congregations to reappropri-ate their common roots.[4] Spirituality has experienced a similar convergence. Rediscovering the forms of prayer, meditation, and Scripture study used in the early church has breathed new life into the spiritual practices of our time. Many Protestants have experienced unexpected meaning through the use of icons, the daily office, and even the rosary.

The danger to both worship and spirituality is that openness and breadth will lead to a shallow dilettantism that seeks one more new experience rather than a deeper relationship with God. The exploration of alternative tradi-tions and practices must be balanced by a reclaiming of one's native spiritual heritage if it is to have genuineness and authenticity. People's own traditions often are just as much unexplored territory as are the traditions of others. "What is Reformed spirituality?" is often asked in Reformed churches.

TRADITION IN THE REFORMED TRADITION

Tradition is self-defining in the sense that judgments about what is the tradition themselves become part of the tradition. The churches of the Reformation attacked much of the accumulated tradition of Roman Catholicism as unscriptural. "Therefore, we do not admit any other judge than God himself, who proclaims by the Holy Scriptures what is true, what is false, what is to be followed, or what is to be avoided," says the Second Helvetic Confession (*BC* 5.013). This has put the Reformed churches in the moderately ironic position of having a suspicion of tradition be a part of their tradition. This is not at all a rejection of tradition, but it is a scrutiny of it. The principle of judgment is whether or not any instantiation of tradition, such as a creed, is an accurate reflection of the teaching of Scripture.

The introduction to the Confession of 1967, repeated in the *Book of Order*, attempts to do justice to the Reformed view of tradition: "Confessions and declarations are subordinate standards in the church, subject to the authority of Jesus Christ, the Word of God, as the Scriptures bear witness to him. No one type of confession is exclusively valid, no one statement is irreformable" (*BC* 9.03; cf. *BO* F-2.02). The term *subordinate standards*, while it might have an oxymoronic ring to it, really is an attempt to locate the place of tradition in the governance and life of the church. The creeds and confessions are to be taken seriously, but not so seriously that they functionally supplant the voice of the living Lord, Jesus Christ, and the witness of the Scripture that proclaims him. The fourth ordination question reflects this: "Will you be a minister of the Word and Sacrament in obedience to Jesus Christ, under the authority of Scripture, and continually guided by our confessions?" The confessions are for *guidance*. We do not promise to obey the confessions as such. We promise to obey Jesus Christ, guided by the confessions. This is not just a matter of formulating doctrines. It is at the heart of the process of using the Reformed tradition as a guide for living rather than as just a summary of beliefs.

LIVING AS A REFORMED CHRISTIAN

In order to see how the Reformed tradition can be a guide for living, we must consider it in the concrete. When we refer to the "Reformed tradition," we are talking about a family of Christian churches with a common history, a shared theology, and a way of living. We will examine each of these.

The Reformed Tradition as History

The Reformed tradition began in Switzerland, shortly after Luther's Reformation began in Germany. In 1517, Luther issued his Ninety-five Theses in response to a campaign to sell indulgences throughout Germany. (He may or may not have nailed these theses to the Wittenberg Cathedral door.) In 1519, a Swiss priest named Ulrich Zwingli began preaching his way through the Gospel of Matthew, calling for ecclesiastical reform as he did so. This was the beginning of the Swiss Reformation.

The Reformed tradition is inextricably (and appropriately) linked with the name of John Calvin. However, reforming activities in Switzerland had been under way for several years before Calvin became involved in the mid-1530s.[5] The centrality of Calvin in the history of the Reformed tradition is due to two primary factors: First, Geneva became a center for reformers from all over Europe during Calvin's lifetime. Second, Calvin's book, *Institutes of the Christian Religion*, became the theological textbook of the Reformed tradition and, in some sense, of the Reformation itself.

The Reformed movement very quickly spread to other countries in Europe and to the newly colonized lands in the Americas. In Europe, warfare between Protestant and Catholic governments erupted and continued sporadically until 1648.[6] In America, Puritans and Congregationalists from England, Presbyterians from Scotland (often via Ireland), and Reformed churches from various European nations formed a somewhat uneasy peace with each other (and with Catholics, Anabaptists, Quakers, and others). The first of a number of revivals—so-called Great Awakenings—erupted in New England in the 1730s. These revivals eventually split almost every denomination in America into prorevival and antirevival factions. This, coupled with the divisive issue of slavery, produced rifts that are only now being healed. The 1983 reunion of the United Presbyterian Church in the U.S.A. and the Presbyterian Church in the U.S. is the latest in a series of reunions and mergers through which Presbyterians are seeking to recover institutional unity. The Brief Statement of Faith, which was added to the *Book of Confessions* in 1991, is both a monument to that reunion and an addition to the Reformed tradition itself.

The Reformed Tradition as Theological Emphases

Although the Reformed tradition has produced an enormous variety of theologies, there are certain constants. As stated in the *Book of Order*, the first of these is as follows: "the affirmation of the majesty, holiness, and providence of God who in Christ and by the power of the Spirit creates, sustains, rules, and redeems the world in the freedom of sovereign righteousness and love" (F-2.05).

This statement is very carefully nuanced. The acknowledgment of God's sovereignty is balanced by an equally strong acknowledgment of God's loving purposes and intentions for redemption and salvation. There is a caricature of the Reformed view of God in which God's sovereignty is stressed at the expense of everything else, so that God becomes a capricious tyrant rather than a benevolent parent. This falsifies both the Bible and the tradition. In the Reformed tradition, God's love is not a check on God's sovereignty. Rather, God's sovereignty is the expression of the power of God's love. The Brief Statement of Faith recalls the language of both Old and New Testaments to underscore this point: "Like a mother who will not forget her nursing child, like a father who runs to welcome the prodigal home, God is faithful still" (BC 10.3, lines 49–51).

The Book of Order adds four other themes of the Reformed tradition to this central affirmation:

1. The election of the people of God for service as well as for salvation.
2. Covenant life marked by a disciplined concern for order in the church according to the Word of God.
3. A faithful stewardship that shuns ostentation and seeks proper use of the gifts of God's creation.
4. The recognition of the human tendency to idolatry and tyranny, which calls the people of God to work for the transformation of society by seeking justice and living in obedience to the Word of God. (BO F-2.05)[7]

The emphasis in each of these themes is the posture of the church in the world. Positively, the church works for a better, more just society; the "service" in the first point is the service of all, not just those in the church. The disciplined order and faithful use of gifts support this work. Resisting idolatry and tyranny overcomes impediments to it. In short, honoring and obeying the sovereign God means that Reformed Christians can and must work within the world for its transformation while remaining free from being subjugated to it. This has enormous consequences for Reformed spirituality.

First, there can be no separation between doctrine, ethics, and spirituality, because there can be no separation between God and God's world. The Reformed Christian can never leave the world or consider a choice for God to be a choice against the world. Loving God means loving the world that God loves and working for its renewal. Second, there can be no confusing or merging of God and God's world. Only by giving God ultimate allegiance and obedience can the Reformed Christian live out an effective and productive freedom in the world. Once the world and God are melded together, freedom disappears and slavery triumphs.

The Theological Declaration of Barmen, from 1934, is both a statement of allegiance to God and of resistance to Adolf Hitler. The six "evangelical truths" of part 2 are carefully formulated so that each truth contains three parts: quotations from Scripture, a theological affirmation based on those quotations, and a rejection of "false doctrine" that denies or contests these affirmations. The sequence is important in that priority is always given to Scripture and all the rejections and denials are based on, and subordinate to, the affirmations. Throughout, the state is simultaneously honored and circumscribed.

While the circumstances that led to the formulation of the Barmen Declaration were very specific, the principles adduced transcend all circumstances. The affirmation of the priority of Jesus Christ, "the one Word of God which we have to hear and which we have to trust and obey in life and in death" (BC 8.11)—the language deliberately echoes the beginning of the Heidelberg Catechism—is beyond circumstance. The task of the state is carefully defined as "providing for justice and peace" (BC 8.22), but that task also sets limits on the state. It cannot become "the single and totalitarian order of human life" (BC 8.23), and neither can the church.

In sum, the theological affirmations that characterize the Reformed tradition lead to a special way of being in the world—a way marked by freedom from the world because of one's commitment to God, coupled with service in the world which that freedom makes possible.[8] An authentic Reformed spirituality can never be one that leaves the world to its own devices, nor can it be an individualistic exercise in pious practices or sentimental emotions. Commitment to God brings one into the world rather than releasing one from it.

The Reformed Tradition as Dutiful Freedom

In the *Book of Confessions*, spirituality and ethics are characteristically treated together, in the context of discussions of the Ten Commandments. Such discussions are found in the three catechisms: Heidelberg, Shorter Westminster, and Larger Westminster.[9] The Larger Westminster Catechism contains the most explicit instruction about how the Ten Commandments are to be understood and used. The Commandments are divided into two parts—the "two tables" of the law. The first table, the first four commandments, specifies our duty toward God and is summarized by the Great Commandment, to love God "with all our heart, and with all our soul, and with all our strength, and with all our mind" (Q. 102, BC 7.212). The second table, our duty toward others, is contained in the last six commandments and is summarized by the requirement "to love our neighbor as ourselves, and to do to others what we would have them do to us" (Q. 122, BC 7.232). This law, which the catechism characterizes as the "moral law," is binding upon all humanity. However, because of the effects of human sinfulness, it cannot be fulfilled. This is the cruel paradox of the law: we are liable for punishment, even eternal punishment, for not doing that which we cannot do. This is what, in some people's view, makes God into a monster.

This issue is central to the New Testament, particularly the writings of Paul, who fights to separate the manifestation of God's grace from conformity to the law.[10] Our justification—originally a legal term that amounts to being declared not guilty—is a sheer, unmerited gift. Humans have nothing to point to, nothing to appeal to, as evidence of innocence. We are guilty. Our salvation is God's work, not our work.

If salvation does not come from the law, why bother with it? What is the point of keeping the legal material in the Old Testament as part of the Christian Bible? Why make children memorize the Ten Commandments?

In *Institutes of the Christian Religion*, John Calvin discusses three uses of the law. First, by demonstrating God's righteousness and the inability of humans to conform to that righteousness, it demonstrates our need for grace. Second, by the threats of punishment and condemnation, it restrains people from acting on their sinful inclinations and desires. In this sense, law is necessary for the working of human society. Third, the law acts as a guide to life, in making God's will explicit and in demonstrating how we can conform ourselves more fully to that will.[11]

This third use of the law became one of the distinctive elements of the Reformed tradition. Even though God's grace is manifested apart from the law, the law still acts as a guide for life. Living according to the moral law is not the precondition for grace; it is the result of grace. It is grace given form. Furthermore, it is not the curtailing of freedom; it is freedom in action.

In the first and the second tables, duties toward God and duties toward others, each of the Ten Commandments requires and prohibits something. Where there is a prohibition, a "You shall not," the opposite of that which is forbidden is required. Where there is a requirement, the opposite of that which is required is forbidden. Consequently, each of the commandments must be read in a double sense. It is not enough simply to refrain from certain acts. One must also work to realize their opposites.[12]

For example, the Sixth Commandment seems straightforward: "You shall not murder" (Exod. 20:13). Clearly, the taking of life is forbidden. But following the principle that when something is forbidden the opposite is required, the Sixth Commandment requires the protection and enhancement of life as well as prohibiting the taking of life. The Larger Westminster Catechism provides a rather daunting list of all that is required and prohibited:

Q. 135. What are the duties required in the Sixth Commandment?

A. The duties required in the Sixth Commandment are: all careful studies and lawful endeavors, to preserve the life of ourselves and others, by resisting all thoughts and purposes, subduing all passions, and avoiding all occasions, temptations, and practices, which tend to the unjust taking away the life of any; by just defense thereof against violence; patient bearing of the hand of God, quietness of mind, cheerfulness of spirit, a sober use of meat, drink, physic, sleep, labor, and recreation; by charitable thoughts, love, compassion, meekness, gentleness, kindness; peaceable, mild, and courteous speeches and behavior, forbearance, readiness to be reconciled, patient bearing and forgiving of injuries, and requiting good for evil; comforting and succoring the distressed, and protecting and defending the innocent.

Q. 136. What are the sins forbidden in the Sixth Commandment?

A. The sins forbidden in the Sixth Commandment are: all taking away the life of ourselves, or of others, except in case of public justice, lawful war, or necessary defense; the neglecting or withdrawing the lawful or necessary means of preservation of life; sinful anger, hatred, envy, desire of revenge; all excessive passions; distracting cares; immoderate use of meat, drink, labor, and recreation; provoking words; oppression, quarreling, striking, wounding, and whatsoever else tends to the destruction of the life of any. (BC 7.245–46).

Some have read this as replacing one commandment with innumerable others and have charged the catechism with a return to an excessive legalism in which the various requirements and prohibitions involved in the commandments are too many even to remember, let alone fulfill. This seems to me to be a misunderstanding. Rather than being an expansion of the Commandments from ten to hundreds, the duties and prohibitions illustrate what is really involved in keeping a commandment.

Consequently, different times and circumstances would result in different duties and prohibitions. Today, there is enormous concern about the deterioration of our physical environment due to overpopulation, pollution, and sheer wastefulness on a massive scale. Some have begun to wonder if we are making the earth uninhabitable. Today, the Sixth Commandment might be applied to the planet itself, as well as the living beings that inhabit it. The requirement "to preserve the life of ourselves and others" means to live in responsible and sustainable ways, destroying as little as possible and nourishing as much as possible. The practice of recycling might not seem at first to be a way of observing the Sixth Commandment, but seen from this perspective, it is. The Westminster Divines (to give them the customary honorific) could not have foreseen this, but they provided the basic principle that allowed them in their time, and we in ours, to apply the law validly to diverse circumstances.

The Sixth Commandment is part of the second table of the law, which is concerned with our duty toward our neighbors. The commandments that form the first table—our duty toward God—are treated in the same way. With the First Commandment, "I am the Lord your God, who brought you out of the land of Egypt, out of the house of slavery; you shall have no other gods before me" (Exod. 20:2–3), a long list of duties and prohibitions is adduced in explanation of this commandment. Again, rather than being additional individual requirements and proscriptions, they are specifications that enable us to see what is really involved in following this (seemingly simple) commandment:

Q. 104. What are the duties required in the First Commandment?

A. The duties required in the First Commandment are: the knowing and acknowledging of God to be the only true God, and our God; and to worship and glorify him accordingly; by thinking, meditating, remembering, highly esteeming, honoring, adoring, choosing, loving, desiring, fearing of him; believing him; trusting, hoping, delighting, rejoicing in him; being zealous for him; calling upon him, giving all praise and thanks, and yielding all obedience and submission to him with the whole man; being careful in all things to please him, and sorrowful when in anything he is offended; and walking humbly with him.

Q. 105. What are the sins forbidden in the First Commandment?

A. The sins forbidden in the First Commandment are: atheism, in denying or not having a God; idolatry, in having or worshiping more gods than one, or any with, or instead of the true God; the not having and vouching him for God, and our God; the omission or neglect of anything due to him, required in this commandment; ignorance, forgetfulness, misapprehensions, false opinions, unworthy and wicked thoughts of him; bold and curious searchings into his secrets; all profaneness, hatred of God, self-love, self-seeking, and all other inordinate and immoderate setting of our mind, will, or affections upon other things, and taking them off from him in whole or in part; vain credulity, unbelief, heresy, misbelief, distrust, despair, incorrigibleness, and insensibleness under judgments, hardness of heart, pride, presumption, carnal security, tempting of God; using unlawful means, and trusting in lawful means; carnal delights and joys, corrupt, blind, and indiscreet zeal; lukewarmness, and deadness in the things of God; estranging ourselves, and apostatizing from God; praying or giving any religious worship to saints, angels, or any other creatures; all compacts and consulting with the devil, and hearkening to his suggestions; making men the lords of our faith and conscience;

slighting and despising God, and his commands; resisting and grieving of his Spirit, discontent and impatience at his dispensations, charging him foolishly for the evils he inflicts on us; and ascribing the praise of any good, we either are, have, or can do, to fortune, idols, ourselves, or any other creature. (*BC* 7.214–15)

Initially, it might be hard to see in this anything other than an arcane and slightly archaic list of dos and don'ts that are impossible to keep in our heads, let alone our lives. Finally, though, all this is about freedom. There is no harsher taskmaster than a false god; our creations and fantasies do not rule us with benevolence.

The purpose of Christian liberty, according to the Westminster Confession of Faith, is that "we might serve the Lord without fear, in holiness and righteousness before him, all the days of our lives" (*BC* 6.110). Such freedom is compromised, and possibly obliterated, when that which we serve is something other than the Lord. The prophet Isaiah stresses this point when he contrasts the labor of those who carry idols with the God who carries them:

> These things you carry are loaded
>   as burdens on weary animals.
> They stoop, they bow down together;
>   they cannot save the burden,
>   but themselves go into captivity.
> Listen to me, O house of Jacob,
>   all the remnant of the house of Israel,
> who have been borne by me from your birth,
>   carried from the womb;
> even to your old age I am he,
>   even when you turn gray I will carry you.
> I have made, and I will bear;
>   I will carry and will save.
>
>   (Isa. 46:1–4)

In serving God, we do not serve a dead thing, a created thing, or an arrogant and arbitrary being. We serve the one who serves, and that service is our liberation from domination by dead things, created things, and arrogant and arbitrary powers.

The "recognition of the human tendency to idolatry and tyranny," the fourth of the great themes of the Reformed tradition, is grounded in this understanding of the First Commandment. It calls for a special kind of discernment, a special alertness to the possibility of false gods around us. These gods do not always have names like Bel or Nebo. Their names can be Power, Wealth, or Pleasure. To paraphrase Augustine of Hippo, the issue is the ability to distinguish between what should be loved and what should be used.

When we love those things that should only be used, we are tending toward idolatry, and we threaten the First Commandment.

This then is the dutiful freedom of the Reformed tradition. Freed from regarding observance of the law (any law) as the condition of salvation, the Reformed Christian can use God's law as a protocol for a life of loving service. The law is similar to the outlined footprints on the floor of a dance class: to learn where our feet go is necessary for the dance, but this does not inhibit the art and joy of dancing; it makes it possible. In dancing the Christian life, we become who we really are.

TRADITION IN UNTRADITIONAL TIMES

The Reformed tradition is a history, a theology, and a way of living. The history began in sixteenth-century Switzerland and spread around the world. The theology, in its many articulations across four centuries, strives both to honor God and to continually reform itself and its church. The way of living uses the law as a guide for a life of dutiful freedom. Taken together, the history, the theology, and the way of living form a valid way of being a Christian. At their best, Christians shaped by the Reformed tradition are devoted to God, suspicious of all idols, and freely active in the world according to law.

Tradition comes into its own in untraditional times. When cultures and communities, including communities of faith, become stereotyped and stale, a rebellion against tradition is appropriate and almost inevitable; human creativity and spontaneity will demand new ways of thinking and acting. But in times that are more chaotic and formless than patterned and predictable, tradition becomes a guide. It is more like a compass than like the walls of a tightly enclosed room.

Spirituality, in modern parlance, often implies a rejection of tradition, or rather a rejection of any single tradition in favor of an eclectic stew of whatever elements of various religions one finds appealing or attractive. Often, though, people will find the guidance they seek by deepening their tradition rather than abandoning it. The two questions of the human search, "Where is my place in the world?" and "Who am I really?" cannot be answered directly by any tradition or combination of traditions, since each individual is something new in the universe and each individual's circumstances break free from previous patterns. But the questions, or rather the exploration of the questions, can be guided by tradition. In saying, "This is what God is and is not," "This is what has come before you," and "This is what to do with human freedom," the Reformed tradition gives guidance to the living of life.

QUESTIONS FOR COMPREHENSION
AND SELF-EXPLORATION

1. Do you have a faith tradition? What about it is important to you? Is there anything that you reject?
2. From your point of view, what does the Reformed tradition offer to those seeking to live as a Christian?
3. Are there other Christian traditions or even other religions that you find attractive or helpful? What are they? What about them do you value?

Interlude

"These Three"

Faith, Hope, and Love

"And now faith, hope, and love abide, these three," Paul wrote to the Christians at Corinth, "and the greatest of these is love" (1 Cor. 13:13). He was fond of this triad and referred to it twice in his first letter to a group of Christians in Thessalonica: at the beginning ("We always give thanks to God for all of you and mention you in our prayers, constantly remembering before our God and Father your work of faith and labor of love and steadfastness of hope in our Lord Jesus Christ"; 1 Thess. 1:2–3) and at the end of the letter ("But since we belong to the day, let us be sober, and put on the breastplate of faith and love, and for a helmet the hope of salvation; 1 Thess. 5:8). Faith, hope, and love are the characteristics of the Christian.

When Augustine of Hippo (354–430) was asked to write a little handbook about the Christian faith, he organized it according to faith, hope, and love. Under these headings he was able to discuss "what we are to believe, what we are to hope for, and what we are to love."[1] Augustine's exposition of faith follows a version of the Apostles' Creed, the customary way of instructing candidates for baptism in the early church.[2] His discussion of hope, which is much briefer, refers to the petitions of the Lord's Prayer as the substance of the eternal and temporal things we hope for. The concluding exposition on love, which is also very brief, maintains that love is the purpose or goal of the Ten Commandments. Thus, Augustine associates faith, hope, and love with three of the foundational documents of the Christian faith.

This pattern can be seen in the three catechisms in the *Book of Confessions* (Heidelberg, Shorter Westminster, and Larger Westminster) as well as the Study Catechism of 1998. What is to be believed (faith) is demonstrated by the Apostles' Creed; what is to be asked (hope) is modeled by the Lord's Prayer; and what is to be loved is specified by the Ten Commandments, of which the two great commandments are a summary. To learn the Apostles' Creed, the Lord's Prayer, and the Ten Commandments is to learn the Christian faith.

This is true for individuals, but it is also true for the church as such. The Creed, the Prayer, and the Commandments express the faith, hope, and love of the body of Christ. The prominence of the Apostles' Creed and Lord's Prayer, and in some cases the Ten Commandments, in the liturgy highlight this.[3] The assembled congregation reciting these texts represents more than a concordance of individual expressions, still less a form of coerced ecclesial conformity. It is the church declaring what it believes, hopes, and does precisely because it is the body of Christ. Individual beliefs undoubtedly waver, individual prayers falter, and individual obedience varies. But the church is always more than the sum total of individuals. It is, according to 1 Corinthians 12:12, the body of Christ, united with and by the Spirit. It would be impossible to maintain that the church itself never wavers, falters, or varies in its obedience; history would argue otherwise. It is true, however, that the church can allow for and accommodate these individual variations while maintaining a continuous witness.

Faith, hope, and love do not just imply a "what." They also imply a "who." They indicate a double relationship. Faith is not only what we believe; it is also whom we believe. Hope is not only what we are to ask for; it is also whom we are to ask. Love is not only our duty to God and our neighbor; it is our response to the One who loves us and who gives us the capacity to love our neighbor.

The Reformed tradition has insisted not only that is God present in our believing, our hoping, and our loving, but that God has the priority. Faith is preceded by grace, hope is preceded by promise, and love is preceded by love. Faith, hope, and love are the human responses to God's acts. Furthermore, the Reformed tradition also teaches that sin has so distorted and incapacitated our ability to respond that divine healing is necessary before we can respond at all. It is not as though we are sick and too weak to respond. It is as though we are dead. God's grace is more than healing. It is more like resurrection.

In the remaining chapters, we will follow the pattern of the catechisms, discussing Reformed spirituality from the aspects of faith, hope, and love. In this discussion, we will see that faith, hope, and love are not three different things. They are one thing—our response to God's grace—seen three different ways. We will be keeping three questions in view for each of these three ways of responding: What is it? How does it arise and develop? What spiritual disciplines flow from it? We will use the *Book of Confessions* as our primary teacher, but we will also draw from other themes and concepts in the life and teaching of the church. Throughout, our aim will be to better learn of and follow after the God who is our God, "to whom alone we must cleave, whom alone we must serve, whom only we must worship, and in whom alone we put our trust" (*BC* 3.01).

QUESTIONS FOR COMPREHENSION
AND SELF-EXPLORATION

1. Why are the Apostles' Creed, the Ten Commandments, and the Lord's Prayer summarized by faith, love, and hope?
2. Paul writes, "And now faith, hope, and love abide, these three; and the greatest of these is love" (1 Cor. 13:13). Do you agree? Why might love be the greatest? How might you argue that faith or hope is the greatest?

4

Faith

FAITH: ASSENT WITH AN ATTITUDE

The word *faith* is commonly used in at least three ways: to indicate that we believe, to indicate what we believe, and to indicate why we believe. A statement such as "I have faith that the world is round" says that we believe something to be true. "I have faith that . . ." and "I believe that . . ." are roughly synonymous—not as strong as "I know that . . ." but much stronger than "I wonder if . . ." or "probably . . ." Such statements do not say why we believe or what evidence we might have. They just say that we think something is true.

A statement like this, "I have faith in John," is different. It says more than that we believe the person named John exists. It says that John is the kind of person who inspires confidence and trust. "I believe John because I have faith in him" is a statement that tells why we believe.

A statement such as "I am an adherent of the Christian faith" indicates what we believe. The term *Christian faith* points to a system of belief that is also a way of life—in short, a religion. The first line of the sixth-century Athanasian Creed, "Whoever wants to be saved must, before everything else, hold the catholic faith," uses the word in this sense.[1]

In the documents that make up the *Book of Confessions*, faith means more than the fact that we believe or the content of what we believe. Faith in God is not just believing that there is a supreme being. It is trusting in God; it is entrusting one's life to the trustworthy God.

The Brief Statement of Faith, the newest of the documents in the *Book of Confessions*, emphasizes this point. Each of its three major sections begins with the phrase "We trust in . . . ," followed by a person of the Trinity. The Brief Statement emphasizes that the Reformed understanding of faith contains both a believing *in* and a believing *that*. We believe that certain things are true: God created the world, Jesus died on the cross, the Spirit binds us together in the church. We believe in God the Father, Christ the Son, and the Holy Spirit. *Believing that* is assent to the witness of Scripture. *Believing in* is the attitude of trust.

Assent to what?

The confessional documents agree that faith involves both knowledge and trust. The definition in the Heidelberg Catechism is typical:

> Q. 21. What is true faith?
>
> A. It is not only a certain knowledge by which I accept as true all that God has revealed to us in his Word, but also a wholehearted trust which the Holy Spirit creates in me through the gospel, that, not only to others, but to me also God has given the forgiveness of sins, everlasting righteousness and salvation, out of sheer grace solely for the sake of Christ's saving work.
>
> Q. 22. What, then, must a Christian believe?
>
> A. All that is promised us in the gospel, a summary of which is taught us in the articles of the Apostles' Creed, our universally acknowledged confession of faith. (*BC* 4.021–4.022)

Thus, the knowledge to which Christians assent comes from God through Scripture and is summarized by creeds, notably the Apostles' Creed. The importance of the Creed in this respect is not that it comes from the apostles (which it does not, at least not directly) or that it is a means of revelation in addition to Scripture. Its validity and authority come only because it is an accurate summary of the central truths of Scripture: "The catholic faith is not given to us by human laws, but by the Holy Scriptures, of which the Apostles' Creed is a compendium" (Second Helvetic Confession, *BC* 5.141). The truth of the Apostles' Creed depends on the truth of Scripture, rather than being another source of truth alongside Scripture.

The Apostles' Creed is much more about what God does than what God is. Certain of the terms are Trinitarian: *Father, Son*, and *Holy Spirit*. But most of this creed is narrative. The Father acts to create ("Maker of heaven and earth"), the Son acts to redeem ("who was conceived . . . born . . . suffered . . . died . . .was buried . . . rose . . . ascended . . . shall come"), and the Spirit acts to sustain and renew (that which follows "I believe in the Holy Ghost" denotes the realm and result of the Spirit's activity).[2] This is very simple in comparison to the rest of the documents in the *Book of Confessions*, with the possible exception of the Brief Statement of Faith. There is no series of superlative adjectives to describe God, such as is found at the beginning of the Westminster Confession:

> There is but one only living and true God, who is infinite in being and perfection, a most pure spirit, invisible, without body, parts, or passions, immutable, immense, eternal, incomprehensible, almighty; most wise, most holy, most free, most absolute, working all things according to the counsel of his own immutable and most righteous will, for his own glory; most loving, gracious, merciful, long-suffering, abundant in goodness and truth, forgiving iniquity, transgression, and sin. (*BC* 6.011)

The language of the Westminster Confession might be in accord with the Bible, and many biblical references are attached to it, but it is not the biblical language as such. Westminster (and the Second Helvetic Confession is similar) begins with a rather abstract philosophical description of God. In the Apostles' Creed, by contrast, the focus is almost entirely on the work of salvation.

The summary of Scripture that the Apostles' Creed presents, then, is the story of God acting to save God's creation from the consequences of human sin. Much of that story has to do with the establishment and history of a particular people, the nation of Israel. Some of it has to do with what to expect, in terms of God's final triumph. Some of it has to do with a particular individual, Jesus of Nazareth, and those who followed him. And that is the heart of the matter.

Trust in Whom?

The New Testament tells stories about Jesus. It also makes statements about Jesus. The stories and the statements reflect each other and depend on each other, but they are quite different. Take these examples:

A Story about Jesus

Again he entered the synagogue, and a man was there who had a withered hand. They watched him to see whether he would cure him on the sabbath, so that they might accuse him. And he said to the man who had the withered hand, "Come forward." Then he said to them, "Is it lawful to do good or to do harm on the sabbath, to save life or to kill?" But they were silent. He looked around at them with anger; he was grieved at their hardness of heart and said to the man, "Stretch out your hand." He stretched it out, and his hand was restored. The Pharisees went out and immediately conspired with the Herodians against him, how to destroy him. (Mark 3:1–6)

A Statement about Jesus

He is the image of the invisible God, the first-born of all creation; for in him all things in heaven and on earth were created, things visible and invisible, whether thrones or dominions or rulers or powers—all things have been created through him and for him. He himself is before all things, and in him all things hold together. He is the head of the body, the church; he is the beginning, the firstborn from the dead, so that he might come to have first place in everything. For in him all the fullness of God was pleased to dwell, and through him God was pleased to reconcile to himself all things, whether on earth or in heaven, by making peace through the blood of his cross. (Col. 1:15–20)

Comparing these passages, we can certainly conclude that what Jesus did and who Jesus was have something to do with each other. We might conclude that Jesus was able to do what he did, namely, heal the man with the with-ered hand, because of who he was—the one in whom God dwelt and through whom God worked. We might also see that there are three types of responses to Jesus. There was the man who held out his withered hand to be healed, there were the Pharisees who plotted against him, and there were the onlook-ers who watched.

Even though these two passages are quite different, they support each other. The story from Mark can be used to supply evidence that Jesus was the person that the Colossians passage says he was. The Colossians passage can help us interpret Mark's story properly, so that we understand this healing to be the work and will of God, and one instance of the reconciliation of all things.

But what about our spiritual life? How does the story about what Jesus did and the passage about who Jesus was affect us here and now? If we remember that one of the central questions we ask ourselves is, "Who am I really?" we can examine whether or not anyone in the story is like us. Are we the man with the withered hand, wounded and looking to Jesus for healing? Are we like the Pharisees and Herodians, seeing Jesus as a dangerous threat to us? Or are we one of the people in the crowd, watching with interest but not committing to anything? Are we in some way like Jesus, doing what we can to offer healing and hope? Or are we, at one time or another, and in one way or another, all of these?

In short, this story tells us something about Jesus. But it also tells us something about ourselves. It tells us who we are in relation to Jesus. It tells us about our faith. It tells us whether or not our belief *that* Jesus was a certain kind of person—the one in whom God dwelt fully—is accompanied by belief *in* Jesus, the one we can trust with our lives.

The Apostles' Creed contains the same double nature. It moves back and forth from statement to story, from who God and Christ are to what they do:

Who God Is	[I believe in] God the Father Almighty
What God Does	Maker of heaven and earth
Who Jesus Christ Is	[and in Jesus Christ] his only Son our Lord
What Jesus Christ Does	who was conceived by the Holy Ghost, born of the Virgin Mary, suffered under Pontius Pilate, was crucified, dead, and buried; he descended into hell; the third day he rose again from the dead; he ascended into heaven, and sitteth on the right hand of God the Father Almighty; from thence he shall come to judge the quick and the dead.

In the third article, the Apostles' Creed simply says, "I believe in the Holy Ghost," followed by a series related to the church and the future—by implication, what the Holy Spirit does. The Nicene Creed is more explicit about the nature and work of the Spirit:

Who the Holy Spirit Is	[We believe in the Holy Spirit] the Lord,
What the Holy Spirit Does	the giver of life who proceeds from the Father and the Son, who with the Father and the Son is worshiped and glorified, who has spoken through the prophets.

The Apostles' and Nicene Creeds thus reflect Scripture, in which the nature and the activity of the triune God are declared and recounted. The statements about God tell us the nature of the God in whom we trust; the history of God's acts demonstrate why God is trustworthy. In the process of learning these creeds, repeating them in the worship of the church, and relating them to the Scripture that they summarize, we find our place in the story and thereby our identity and our role as Christian disciples.

HOW FAITH DEVELOPS

According to the Heidelberg Catechism, we must know three things in the life of faith: "First, the greatness of my sin and wretchedness. Second, how I am freed from all my sins and their wretched consequences. Third, what gratitude I owe to God for such redemption" (Q. 1, *BC* 4.002). How does this knowledge come about?

In contemporary times, the theologian-turned-psychologist James W. Fowler has conducted extensive research into the process of faith development.[3] Fowler's work is probably not directly known by many outside of his field of study, but it is almost certain that many of you have encountered it indirectly. Fowler's work has influenced the way Sunday school materials are prepared and the way Christian education specialists teach.

Briefly, Fowler argues that there are six separate stages of faith development that human beings go through, although very few make it all the way to stage 6. These stages hold even for people of different cultures and religions. They are not specifically Christian, but describe the way human beings find something in which to believe.

Fowler describes in detail how people pass from an initial childhood stage in which faith is akin to fantasy, to the various ways adults appropriate and understand their system of beliefs. The important thing for our purposes is that Fowler argues that having faith in something outside oneself is a part of what it means to be human. The objects of faith may—and do—vary considerably, but the fact of faith remains constant in human life.

What you believe in does make a difference, however. At this point, we go beyond anything that can be said by social scientists who study religion. Social science can describe how people develop their beliefs, but it cannot speak about the work of the Holy Spirit in that development, which is the most crucial work of all. All we can do as human beings is cooperate with the work that God does within us. As Paul says, "But by the grace of God I am what I am, and his grace toward me was not in vain. On the contrary, I worked harder than any of them, though it was not I, but the grace of God which is with me" (1 Cor. 15:10).

Through grace, God leads us from the point where we *have* faith to where we *are* faithful. This work is always unfinished within us, for faithfulness must be renewed day by day. Nevertheless, there are stages to this faith. These stages have been described in many ways throughout the history of the church, often involving an image of going upward or inward: climbing a ladder, ascending a mountain, walking through a castle, climbing with eagle's wings. Whatever the image used, however, there are usually three broad movements: purgation, or interior cleansing; illumination, or new knowledge about God, the self, and the world; and union, or becoming one with God.[4] Sometimes these movements occur one after the other. Sometimes they are almost simultaneous. Regardless of the timing, we need to be able to recognize them if we are to understand our own road of faith.

There is no single way that faith begins in a particular human's life. Some people are raised in a particular faith and never leave it. They might have times of broadening or deepening, they might drift into and out of active participation, they might have moments of insight or renewal or recommitment. But whatever the degree of fervor or involvement, their faith is a constant in their lives, and they have never really been without it.

Other people experience a conversion, a "turning around." For them, there is a definite "before" and "after" in their religious life, a distinct time at which they made a decision, a commitment, or a vow. This moment might be marked by a rite or sacrament, or it might be purely internal—a movement of one's mind or heart that changed one's life. It might occur in a group or in solitude. It might be a response to a call, or it might come entirely by surprise.

It is not at all uncommon for people whose religious life has been a constant and people who have experienced a conversion to have difficulty understanding each other. People who have had a single moment of conversion or decision sometimes regard the faith of those who have not had one as inferior or unreal. People whose faith has always been part of their lives might consider those who have had conversion experiences as arrogant or pharisaical. The result can be a dissension that splits congregations or leads people to seek other religious communities. In fact, the history of most denominations in the United States is marked by quarrels and splits over the issues of conversions and revivals.

The history of the early church is not marked by such quarrels. In the first centuries of the church's life, people were much more interested in how faith ended than in how it began. Would a person who had turned to Christ and joined the church remain faithful unto death? Would such a person stand firm in the face of torture and death? If such a person did not stand firm, but denied Christ and offered sacrifice to the Roman emperor, would he or she be allowed to remain in or rejoin the church, and if so, under what conditions? These were the issues the early church faced. Resolving these issues led to an understanding in which grace was primarily conferred through the sacraments of the church, irrespective of the holiness of the priest or bishop who administered them or the person who received them. In the Middle Ages, those people who experienced a definite conversion often were the founders of new religious orders, as in the case of St. Benedict of Nursia and St. Francis of Assisi, or were classed as heretics, such as Peter Waldo, whose followers were known as Waldensians.

During the Reformation, Protestants directed much of their attack at the sacramental system. They argued that five of the seven sacraments of Roman Catholic theology were not sacraments, and rethought the remaining two—baptism and the Lord's Supper—so as to emphasize the priority of God's grace over every human act, and the necessity for faith as the human response over and above every kind of good work.

The churches of the Reformed tradition were particularly susceptible to dissension and division over the issue of revivalism because of a tension in their theology. On the one hand, they stressed that the grace of God was a primordial decision made without consideration of any kind of merit or worth. On the other hand, they stressed belief and trust as the proper and necessary response to the sacrament. This tension is apparent in the Westminster Confession: "This effectual call is of God's free and special grace alone, not from anything at all foreseen in man, who is altogether passive therein, until, being quickened and renewed by the Holy Spirit, he is thereby enabled to answer this call, and to embrace the grace offered and conveyed in it" (*BC* 6.065).

On the one hand, the priority of God's action is emphasized. On the other hand, answering and embracing the grace offered are human acts. It is the grace of God that makes such acts possible; this is a theme throughout the Westminster Confession and the rest of the *Book of Confessions* as well. It is almost impossible to accept this, however, without beginning an intense introspection to determine whether or not one shows evidence of this answering and embracing, and hence evidence that one is among the elect. In short, people started to look for works in their lives that would demonstrate they were saved without works. An experience of conversion could become such a workless work and lead to a Pharisaism of religious experience.

In the face of this, many of the so-called mainline denominations have tended to shy away from any emphasis on conversion. It is either assumed by the fact that one is willing (or was willing) to make a confession of faith, or it is equated with catechetical instruction. While evangelical or conservative denominations seem to focus most of their attention on conversion experiences, conversion in the mainline churches seems not quite nice to talk about.

Yet there undoubtedly is talk about conversion in the *Book of Confessions*, and the Bible itself certainly speaks of it. So what, in the Reformed understanding, is conversion? Or to use language more in keeping with the *Book of Confession*'s own vocabulary, what characterizes the beginning of faith?

First, faith is the work of the Holy Spirit. It is beyond human achievement or even human desire. In short, it is out of one's power to generate one's own faith. On the other hand, even to desire faith is already to demonstrate the presence of faith, for the desire itself is the work of the Spirit, as the passage from the Westminster Confession just cited demonstrates. The upshot is that the one who is genuinely seeking God, under whatever name and by whatever means, is living in a grace-filled world. This does not mean that the seeking is easy. It does mean that the seeking is not futile. The prayer of Psalm 27—"Your face, Lord, do I seek. Do not hide your face from me" (Ps. 27:8–9)—is its own answer, for this prayer cannot be prayed unless the Spirit is at work.

The result is insight into one's true self. The mark of conversion is that one sees oneself anew. The sight is not always pretty. Sometimes it is dismaying. But it is necessary for spiritual health, just as accurate diagnosis is necessary for physical health. Insight into our own sinfulness is itself a gift of grace, as is the desire to do something about it.

Whether it comes as the result of a sudden catharsis or a quiet decision, or in the numerous other ways by which people form a commitment to God, conversion is always some kind of turning: a turning toward the Spirit that is already at work in and around a person, and a turning away from the sin that is recognized as a result of the Spirit's work. This turning away has been called the stage of purgation, or catharsis, or repentance; the turning toward is illumination or sanctification.

STAGES OF FAITH

Purgation

Purgation is the phase in which we recognize our sin and repent over it. It has to do with the first of the three things we must know, according to the Heidelberg Catechism: the greatness of our sin and wretchedness. The goal is to not only recognize the ways we have turned away from or rebelled against God, but also to repudiate all those things in our lives that block or diminish our contact with God. This is the point at which our joy over finding the God who is our God is mixed with our own distress over what we have become.

The Second Helvetic Confession describes four aspects to repentance:

> By repentance we understand (1) the recovery of a right mind in sinful man awakened by the Word of the Gospel and the Holy Spirit, and received by true faith, by which the sinner immediately acknowledges his innate corruption and all his sins accused by the Word of God; and (2) grieves for them from his heart, and not only bewails and

frankly confesses them before God with a feeling of shame, but also
(3) with indignation abominates them; and (4) now zealously considers the amendment of his ways and constantly strives for innocence
and virtue in which conscientiously to exercise himself all the rest of
his life. (*BC* 5.093)

The language of this section might express more emotion than we actually
feel at any given time; contemporary humans tend to be rather sanguine about
their own sinfulness. We do not truly understand ourselves as sinners until
we understand the damage we do and the pain we cause through our sin.
Hatred, arrogance, selfishness, willingness to resort to violence, surrender-
ing self-control to addicting and intoxicating substances, and dozens of other
behaviors are manifestations of sin, but often we do not see them as such (or
we minimize them) until we see their consequences. The purgative stage of
spiritual development comes when we see how it is with us—who we truly are
and what we truly have done—and find the will to change. It is when we realize the consequences of our sin in the world and in the lives of those we love
that we truly grieve over ourselves.

Sometimes this involves ridding ourselves of ways of life that are harmful.
Addictions, abusive behaviors, and disordered appetites all must be identified
and attacked. Twelve-step programs are, in fact, modern variants on hallowed
spiritual disciplines designed to lead us through the purgative way. Our purgation, our cleansing, often involves changing how we deal with the ordinary
things of life. We need the things of this world—food, shelter, clothing. We
need ways of earning our living. We need all sorts of tools and implements
to do the work we do. All these things are good and necessary. But if concern
over them or attachment to them hinders our way to God, we need to change
those concerns and attachments. To use things is good. To love the things we
use can become evil.

There can be enormous pain in this way of purgation, for we often must
give up attachments we have formed. Ultimately we will be healthier, however, because those attachments were holding us down and sapping our
strength. We often feel God's strength precisely at the point where our own
runs out. That is the joy of purgation, the joy of finding that God is truly with
us, giving us his strength when we need it.

Illumination

The second stage, illumination, is concerned with coming to know God. We
attend to God's word. We spend time in prayer. We look around us to see
God's work in the world. We actually enter into conversation with God at
this point. The counterpoint of prayer and Scripture, our speaking to God

and God's speaking to us, forms a pattern to our lives. This pattern nourishes our faith. We learn that we truly are related to God, that God knows us and prepares our way before us.

Illumination is the *turning toward* that corresponds to the *turning away from* of purgation. In fact, there is no purgation without illumination, for every turning is simultaneously a turning away from darkness toward light—a turning from sin to faith, from doubt to trust, from self-obsession to self-giving. The fourth aspect of repentance, in the language of the passage from the Second Helvetic Confession just quoted, describes what illumination really is: amending our ways and striving for innocence and virtue.

This is lifelong work. While purgation and illumination are sometimes presented as discrete stages, with purgation preceding illumination and ending when illumination begins, people seem to more often experience them as alternating movements in the ongoing pattern of life. They seem to be logically and emotionally dependent on each other: purgation requires the discernment given through illumination in order to know what must be purged, and illumination necessitates purgation if it is to have any discernable effect in our lives. This roughly corresponds to the knowledge of God and knowledge of ourselves that Calvin says are the two inseparable parts of human wisdom.[5]

The movement from purgation to illumination, or knowledge of God and knowledge of self, does not simply happen. If it is to be more than an episodic curiosity in one's life, it must be motivated and guided by spiritual practices that aid the acquisition and application of knowledge of God and self. We will examine some of these practices in the next section.

Night

About a decade after Heinrich Bullinger composed the Second Helvetic Confession, Juan de Yepes Alvarez, better known as St. John of the Cross, was composing some of the greatest works in the history of Christian spirituality. One of these works, *Dark Night of the Soul*, named an experience that seems to be almost universal: the feeling of having been abandoned by God.[6]

The spiritual teaching of John of the Cross is its own vast subject, and I will not go into it here. Instead of developing what he meant by *dark night of the soul*, I will use the phrase in a more generic sense to describe the spiritual crises that seem to be a part of the life of anyone who seeks to live in relationship with God.

The beginning of one's spiritual life, the point of turning in which a person decides—or is led to decide—"I will live this way and not that way," is often marked by strong emotion: enthusiasm, rejoicing, gratitude, fervor. It might also be marked by the grieving over oneself described by the Heidelberg

Catechism. In any case, people frequently feel that life is now full of purpose and meaning and hope.

And then? Sometimes the events of life—an illness, a death, a crisis—make one's faith seem pointless and empty. People ask why a loving God would allow such things. Sometimes encounters with other ideas or other religions cause people to question or doubt what they once firmly believed. And sometimes our entire religious life becomes repetitive, stale, and burdensome. A faltering of conviction, a life crisis that leads to a faith crisis, or a loss of purpose and hope—all these experiences and many more can be grouped together as *night*. They mark the points in our life where we encounter the mystery of God.

The Mystery of Circumstances

Events can shake our faith. Sometimes they test our faith. Sometimes they affirm our faith. Sometimes they destroy our faith. This is because such events change who we are. Because we are forced to live our lives differently, our self-understanding becomes different. Illness or injury limits our physical or mental capacities so that we can no longer do things we took for granted. Deaths remove people from us who were central to our world. Job losses, forced relocations, divorces, and countless other crises require us to rebuild our lives. Because we have changed, our relationship to God changes.

These are the times when we are likely to ask, "Why did God allow this?" This question is as natural as it is unanswerable. The Reformed tradition has been insistent that God wills all things, and it has been impatient with distinctions such as the difference between what God determines and what God allows. The Westminster Confession of Faith exemplifies this:

> God, the great Creator of all things, doth uphold, direct, dispose, and govern all creatures, actions, and things, from the greatest even to the least, by his most wise and holy providence, according to his infallible foreknowledge, and the free and immutable counsel of his own will, to the praise of the glory of his wisdom, power, justice, goodness, and mercy. (*BC* 6.024)

To say that God wills all things, however, is not at all to say that God's intentions are discernable through the course of events. To speculate about why God allowed something to happen is inevitably dangerous and often almost blasphemous. Saying that a hurricane struck a city because of its sinfulness, or that a communicable disease is God's punishment for a particular group of people is both irresponsible and irreverent; it is also a violation of the Second Commandment. Attempting to read the mind of God is not a part of the spiritual life. Rather, the spiritual life is concerned with being a vessel that conveys God's grace and compassion to others, especially those others who are experiencing their own dark nights.

The Mystery of Sin

Circumstances are only one way that darkness comes upon us. Recognizing and confronting our own sin is another. The Reformed tradition has always emphasized the gravity and pervasiveness of human sin. It has been shaped by the theology of St. Augustine, who also emphasized the gravity and pervasiveness of human sin, and it confronted a theology in Roman Catholicism that seemed to give undue emphasis to human merit. For these reasons, both Reformed and Lutheran theologians insisted that sin was universal, that it was a matter not just of evil deeds but of an evil orientation in human beings that preceded every deed, and that without God's grace human beings could not do anything whatsoever to overcome (or even desire to overcome) this evil orientation. The language of the Second Helvetic Confession is typical:

> By sin we understand that innate corruption of man which has been derived or propagated in us all from our first parents, by which we, immersed in perverse desires and averse to all good, are inclined to all evil. Full of all wickedness, distrust, contempt and hatred of God, we are unable to do or even to think anything good of ourselves. Moreover, even as we grow older, so by wicked thoughts, words and deeds committed against God's law, we bring forth corrupt fruit worthy of an evil tree (Matt. 12:33ff.). For this reason by our own deserts, being subject to the wrath of God, we are liable to just punishment, so that all of us would have been cast away by God if Christ, the Deliverer, had not brought us back. (*BC* 5.037)

Many want to protest at this point. Such a view is too negative, too depressing. It ignores the fact that many people, perhaps even most people, genuinely do try to live good, honest, productive lives. They love their families, they care for their habitat, they help others when and how they can. Doesn't this emphasis on sin ignore all that? Doesn't it take away the reality of human hopes and human striving?

It is true that the Reformed tradition has sometimes been seen as sin-obsessed and guilt-ridden to the exclusion of everything else. This is a caricature, but it is an understandable caricature. The Reformed tradition truly has emphasized the power of sin, but that theme must be seen in the context of the sovereignty of God's grace. Sin is stronger than any human attempt to withstand or combat it, but it is not stronger than the power of God. In part, the Reformed stress on sin is made not to eliminate hope but to locate it. Hope in any created thing (including the human will to avoid sin) is misplaced, because sin pervades all of creation. But hope in God is well-founded, because God's overcoming of sin is not just a possibility; it is an actuality. It is a fact. Jesus triumphed over sin and death on the cross, and that was and is a real, genuine triumph. It was, as Paul writes in 2 Corinthians—in language that forms the central emphasis of the Confession of 1967—the reconciliation of the world to God: "All this is from God, who reconciled us to himself through Christ, and has given us the ministry of reconciliation; that is, in Christ God was reconciling the world to himself, not counting their trespasses against them, and entrusting the message of reconciliation to us (2 Cor. 5:18–19). Any Reformed understanding of sin must be set in the context of God's triumphant grace. If you know that you are a sinner, you know that you are a forgiven sinner. The Confession of 1967 maintains this sequence: "The reconciling act of God in Jesus Christ exposes the evil in men as sin in the sight of God" (BC 9.12). Sin is only understood as sin in the light of grace.

Having said that, we must be careful not to make sin trivial or abstract. The Confession of 1967 continues, "In sin, men claim mastery of their own lives, turn against God and their fellow men, and become exploiters and despoilers of the world. They lose their humanity in futile striving and are left in rebellion, despair, and isolation." Sin is, in other words, a failure of relationship. It affects all three of the primary human relationships: to God, to others, and to the world. Sin is not simply, or even primarily, a list of forbidden deeds. Sin is anything that distorts or destroys the relationships that define human beings.

The cycle of purgation and illumination depends on this relationship of grace and sin. God's grace exposes sin as sin not only on the cosmic scale, but also within our individual lives. In this sense, our own sinfulness is a matter of revelation, and not just self-knowledge. Even in the light of revelation, however, our own sinfulness remains a mysterious thing.

Sin is a mystery on many levels. Its power is mysterious, for its consequences often go far beyond anything we anticipate. Its very presence is mysterious—how did sin get into God's good creation? And why we continue to succumb to it is mysterious, for most of us do not want to most of the time. Paul's statement in Romans describes all of us: "For I do not do the good I want, but the evil I do not want is what I do" (Rom. 7:19). We do what we do not want to do, and often regret what we are doing even while we do it. Yet we continue to do it.

Ultimately, the grace of God working in us is more like a slow healing than it is a moral renewal. We do have to make decisions. We do have to change our minds. We do have to resolve to act this way and not that way. We do have to make what amends we can for the damage we cause. And it is certainly possible that we do, somehow, get better. But we are never done with our struggle with our own sin. The confessions insist that sanctification is real, that grace produces a genuine improvement in life—but that improvement does not negate or eliminate human sinfulness. In the words of the Westminster Confession of Faith,

> This sanctification is throughout in the whole man, yet imperfect in this life: there abideth still some remnants of corruption in every part, whence ariseth a continual and irreconcilable war, the flesh lusting against the Spirit, and the Spirit against the flesh.
>
> In which war, although the remaining corruption for a time may much prevail, yet, through the continual supply of strength from the sanctifying Spirit of Christ, the regenerate part doth overcome: and so the saints grow in grace, perfecting holiness in the fear of God. (*BC* 6.076-6.077)

Seeing the struggle against sin as a war between flesh and spirit, as Westminster does, certainly has strong precedents in the history of Christian spirituality and in the language of the Bible. But it might create the unfortunate implication that flesh, or matter as such, is evil, and that the nonmaterial is good. The Bible stresses that the material world is not evil at all. It is good. God declared it good. Human beings with human bodies are good. "Subduing the flesh" by means of masochistic "spiritual" exercises is not good. We will see in the next section that there are ways of recognizing and combating our own sinfulness, but those ways involve discernment and trust rather than self-induced pain. They involve a healing of relationships as much as they do a self-contained moral heroism. Sin, in its presence, its power, and its persistence, is a mysterious—malignant, but mysterious—thing. The Christian witness, and the Reformed emphasis, is that God's grace and forgiveness is more present, more powerful, and more persistent than sin.

The Mystery on the Road to God

Of course, not every crisis of life produces a crisis of faith, nor does every instance of sin. Sometimes just the opposite happens: in the midst of crisis, our faith grows stronger; in the midst of sin, we repent. Sometimes we truly manage to incorporate the opening phrases of the Heidelberg Catechism into our lives, and we are indeed "wholeheartedly willing and ready from now on to live for [God]" (Q. 1, *BC* 4.001). Such moments, when they come, can bring incredible consolation and hope. But they might not come very often or last very long.

When St. John of the Cross spoke of the dark night of the soul, he was not thinking primarily of either the mystery of circumstance or the mystery of sin. Rather, he was speaking of the mystery of God and of predictable episodes involved in our relationship with God. Spiritual experience, in John's view, is not always marked by serenity, joy, and peace. Sometimes it involves feelings of abandonment, distress, turmoil, or sheer dullness—the sense that God is absent, one's faith is weak, and the religious life is burdensome and tedious.

In John's understanding, such experiences are not what they seem to be. Rather than the deterioration or loss of faith, they are stages in the growth of faith—the inevitable consequences of breaking one's attachment to created things, or indeed to one's own religiosity, in order to be devoted to God alone.[7]

The *Book of Confessions* occasionally recognizes something similar. In discussing the assurance of salvation, the Westminster Confession acknowledges times of darkness in the Christian life:

> True believers may have the assurance of their salvation divers ways shaken, diminished, and intermitted; as, by negligence in preserving of it; by falling into some special sin, which woundeth the conscience, and grieveth the Spirit; by some sudden or vehement temptation; by God's withdrawing the light of his countenance and suffering even such as fear him to walk in darkness and to have no light: yet are they never utterly destitute of that seed of God, and life of faith, that love of Christ and the brethren, that sincerity of heart and conscience of duty, out of which, by the operation of the Spirit, this assurance may in due time be revived, and by the which, in the meantime, they are supported from utter despair. (*BC* 6.100)

This paragraph certainly teaches us not to confuse our feelings about our faith at any particular time with faith itself. It also points to the role that the church plays in sustaining faith: the "love of Christ and the brethren" is one of our helps in dark times.

What is really going on when we encounter such times? Why is it that our faith can seem weak and illusory to us when we are not experiencing any crisis of circumstance or sin? There are many possibilities, of course, some of which might only be discoverable through some sort of spiritual direction. But one of the possibilities has to do with the very transcendence of God.

The mystery of God is one of the themes of the Bible: "For my thoughts are not your thoughts, nor are your ways my ways, says the LORD. For as the heavens are higher than the earth, so are my ways higher than your ways and my thoughts than your thoughts" (Isa. 55:8–9). God is not a human, and any human terms or concepts we use to try to understand God are approximate at best. Even in God's self-revelation, God remains a mystery.

A provocative passage in Exodus suggests that the hiddenness of God's being is an aspect of God's mercy. In this passage, Moses has asked to see God. This is the reply: "I will make all my goodness pass before you. . . . But . . . you cannot see my face; for no one shall see me and live" (Exod. 33:19–20). The Gospel of John puts it bluntly: "No one has ever seen God" (John 1:18).

God is beyond human comprehension. This does not make God unknowable, but it does mean that God cannot be completely and fully known. God is known because God wills to be known. God is known through the Bible's recounting of God's work, which culminates in the life and teaching of Jesus Christ. "Whoever has seen me has seen the Father," Jesus tells his disciples.

Coming to know Jesus is coming to know God. But this "coming to know" does not dispel the mystery; it locates it. As we saw in chapter 1, the knowledge of God that we gain from Jesus Christ is a very paradoxical sort of knowledge. How can we see the God who is "eternal, infinite, immeasurable, incomprehensible, omnipotent, invisible," as the Scots Confession has it (*BC* 3.01), in the life of an impoverished Galilean itinerant rabbi?

The mystery on the road to God is, in part, the mystery of the one who so utterly transcends us and our world that we have difficulty comprehending and speaking about him. But in greater part it is the mystery of finding that one in and through Jesus Christ. It is the mystery of the finite finding the infinite-in-the-finite. To come closer to that one is, in the words of the early church theologian Gregory of Nyssa, to enter into the divine darkness.

Encountering the mystery on the road to God is not necessarily a matter of anguish. It may be the occasion of profound faith and gratitude, as in the words of the well-known hymn by Walter Chalmers Smith "Immortal, Invisible, God Only Wise": "All praise we would render; O help us to see / 'Tis only the splendor of light hideth Thee."

Because of God's transcendence, we must be very careful about what we think and say. Every statement about God somehow falls short; every concept of God is inadequate. Consequently, we must speak with humility and listen with care, for others will always have something to teach us. We must be aware of the potential for idolatry in our language and ideas. If we become convinced that we have uttered, or are capable of uttering, the final truth about God, our own utterances become idolatrous. Finally, we must always remember that the criterion of correctness in Christian theology is Jesus Christ as Scripture witnesses to him. Faith in Jesus Christ is not simply correct belief about him. It takes the form of trusting obedience to him, even when things seem darkest around us.

Union

The final stage is the stage of union, sometimes called the *unitive way*. This is the stage when we truly find ourselves becoming united to God. We know that God's Holy Spirit dwells within us and that God acts through us. Our awareness of God is more than a passing thought or an occasional apprehension. It is a constant in our lives. This does not imply any extraordinary state of mind or mystical consciousness, nor is it a change of being—we do not become something different than we already are. It is, rather, the stage of spiritual maturity.

Objectively, the union is simply a fact. We are one with Christ because Christ became one with us. In the moving words of the Scots' Confession,

> Since the opposition between the justice of God and our sins was such that no flesh by itself could or might have attained unto God, it behooved the Son of God to descend unto us and take himself a body of our body, flesh of our flesh, and bone of our bone, and so become the Mediator between God and man, giving power to as many as believe in him to be the sons of God. (*BC* 3.08)

The phrase "a body of our body, flesh of our flesh, and bone of our bone" in part emphasizes the fullness of Christ's human nature, but it also testifies to his identification with us and our consequent oneness with him. This is not dependent on anything other than the grace of God. It is neither a reward for nor a response to our faith, our acceptance, our acquiescence, our cooperation, or any other human thing or act. The *Book of Confessions*, and indeed the entire Reformed tradition, insists that the work of salvation, accomplished through Christ's union with us, is entirely God's work.

Subjectively, our knowledge and awareness of this union vary considerably. At times, we may be overwhelmed with the knowledge; at times we may forget it entirely. At times, our belief may be strong, even as our actions contradict our beliefs. It is certainly possible to say "Lord, Lord" with our lips while our deeds say something else entirely.

The two stages we have just been discussing, purgation and illumination, are both consequences of our episodic awareness of our union with Christ: illumination is our realization of who we could and should be; purgation is our acknowledgment of the gap between who we should be and who we are. The stage of union reflects the constancy of this awareness. It is not a repudiation of or departure from the world; it is being in the world in a special way, a way that is constantly open to God's presence. The poem attributed to St. Patrick expresses this awareness:

> Christ be with me, Christ within me,
> Christ behind me, Christ before me,
> Christ beside me, Christ to win me,
> Christ to comfort and restore me,
> Christ beneath me, Christ above me,
> Christ in quiet, Christ in danger,
> Christ in hearts of all that love me,
> Christ in mouth of friend and stranger.[8]

This might also be the lesson of Matthew 25:30–46, the separation of the sheep and the goats. Neither the sheep nor the goats recognized Jesus in those who were strangers, or naked, or ill, or imprisoned. One group responded to the need; the other did not. There is, however, the possibility of a third group: those who responded to the need and *did* see the Lord in the strangers, the naked, the ill, and the imprisoned. That recognition defines the unitive way.

DISCIPLINES OF FAITH

Scripture

One of the fundamental principles of the Reformation was *sola scriptura*, "Scripture alone." The point at issue was not whether or not Scripture conveyed God's revelation. Everyone agreed with that. The point was whether something else conveyed God's revelation alongside Scripture. The "something else" could be an oral tradition, given by Jesus to the disciples but not written; or the Holy Spirit giving new revelations not contained in Scripture; or the church's interpretation of Scripture, which it claimed (or some claimed on its behalf) to be authoritative and binding. In the face of all this, the Reformation insisted that in Scripture God's revelation was given fully and completely. There was no need of and no possibility of any revelation other than that given in Jesus Christ and passed on through Scripture. Nor was there any requirement for an authoritative interpreter of Scripture, such as an ecclesiastical pronouncement. Scripture was self-interpreting. Some parts might be obscure in themselves, but other parts always spoke clearly. Over against the Roman Catholic Church, Protestants insisted that the authority of Scripture was given by God and not dependent on the church. Over against the Anabaptists, Protestants equally insisted that the Holy Spirit did not provide new revelations but instead enabled people to believe and assent to the revelation already given. Accordingly, in the Scots Confession, the Second Helvetic Confession, and the Westminster documents, we find statements about Scripture's authority and sufficiency.[9]

Modern biblical study tends to focus on the circumstances surrounding the composition of the biblical documents and the process by which those documents were collected, edited, and transmitted. One of the purposes of such study is to establish the most reliable text possible; texts can become corrupted as they are handed down through the centuries, and restoring the original is an important and demanding work of scholarship. A second aim of this type of study is to understand the history and cultures of the ancient Israelites and their successors, and their conceptions of the actions of God within that history. Contemporary Christian education depends heavily on the results of this scholarship.

This approach to Scripture, however, has had the unfortunate (and for the most part unintended) result of obscuring the place of the Bible in the spiritual life. How can understanding the history and culture of the ancient Israelites and their successors provide us with "that knowledge of God, and of his will, which is necessary unto salvation" (Westminster Confession of Faith, *BC* 6.001)? Certain portions of Scripture, such as the Ten Commandments and the moral maxims contained in Proverbs, have immediate and straightforward application. Stories such as the crossing of the Red Sea and Daniel in the lions' den can give examples of encouragement and hope. But the relevance of many of the other biblical stories is not immediately obvious, and the commands relating to the total destruction of the Canaanite cities in Joshua are not only confusing but repugnant.

In some respects, these are new versions of old problems. The church has always had difficulty assimilating certain portions of the Old Testament, to the point that certain figures in the early church period suggested that the God of the Old Testament was an entirely different entity than the God who was the Father of Jesus Christ, and that the Old Testament should be jettisoned entirely. The church refused to do this. It insisted that the God of Abraham, Isaac, and Jacob was the Father of Jesus Christ, and that the Old Testament was a valid and trustworthy revelation of that God. It did, however, adopt interpretations of the Old Testament that were dependent on symbolism and allegory, sometimes at the expense of the literal meaning of the text.[10]

At the time of the Reformation, Protestant churches reaffirmed the status of the Old Testament as Scripture, with the exception of several books that were part of the Roman Catholic Bible but were originally written in Greek rather than Hebrew. The list of the books contained in the Bible that begins the Westminster Confession of Faith, which might seem to be an unnecessary belaboring of the obvious, is intended to show both what is retained and what is excluded in the Protestant canon of Scripture.

The Reformers also moved away from the practice of the allegorical interpretation of Scripture. Westminster is explicit in saying that no special exegetical method is required to interpret the key teachings of the Bible:

> All things in Scripture are not alike plain in themselves, nor alike clear unto all; yet those things which are necessary to be known, believed, and observed, for salvation, are so clearly propounded and opened in some place of Scripture or other, that not only the learned, but the unlearned, in a due use of the ordinary means, may attain unto a sufficient understanding of them. (*BC* 6.007)

God's revelation, in other words, was conveyed in ordinary words through ordinary language, and only the ability to read was required to receive and comprehend that revelation. Anything central to Christian faith and life was clearly taught somewhere in Scripture, and what was clear was to govern the interpretation of what was obscure.

This understanding of Scripture, which really is an affirmation of faith in Scripture, holds whether one is thinking of interpretation by ancient allegory or contemporary study of the ancient Near East: the plain sense of Scripture is sufficient to reveal all that is necessary. This is not to deny the helpfulness of the various tools of Bible study, such as dictionaries, commentaries, histories, and handbooks. It is to say that the interpretation of Scripture is not a matter of decoding a secret message. Reading diligently and understanding perceptively are enough. (For a more detailed approach to Scripture reading as a spiritual discipline, see appendix A.)

Prayer

Prayer and Scripture

Prayer and Scripture reading are complementary disciplines. They reflect each other, depend on each other, and strengthen each other. Scripture reading is how we attend to God; prayer is how we respond to God.

We often, perhaps most often, pray out of our own need or the need of someone who is close to us. That is perfectly appropriate and entirely scriptural: "Do not worry about anything, but in everything by prayer and supplication with thanksgiving let your requests be made known to God" (Phil. 4:6). However, in the Reformed understanding, our prayers are first of all an expression of gratitude. The Heidelberg Catechism says that prayer is necessary because "it is the chief part of the gratitude that God requires of us" (Q. 116, BC 4.116). Gratitude is always a response. We cannot be grateful simply because we are told we ought to be grateful. We can only be grateful when we realize that we have received something out of another's benevolence. We can be grateful to God only insofar as we perceive God's love and grace to us.

That is why Scripture reading precedes and enables prayer. The story Scripture tells is the story of God's grace.[11] It recounts God's grace in creating a world that is good, calling a people in that world to be a witness to that world, and becoming a part of that world through the incarnation of Jesus Christ in order to redeem and sanctify it. Our gratitude to God stems from our appreciation for all God has done, which is the principal subject of Scripture. All our asking, whether for ourselves or for others, is in the context of this appreciation.

Prayer in the *Book of Confessions*

Much of the material on prayer in the *Book of Confessions* seems rather polemical. Sometimes it is distressingly polemical because of this basic insight: that prayer stems from gratitude. In the sixteenth and seventeenth centuries—the time of the Scots Confession, the Second Helvetic Confession, the Westminster Confession, and the Heidelberg and Westminster Catechisms, Roman Catholicism was perceived to have abandoned the biblical understanding of prayer (and of grace itself) in favor of a system based on meritorious good works, the intercession of the saints (especially the Virgin Mary), and the church as the dispenser of grace. Contemporary readers need to remember that these confessions come from a particular time, and that the Roman Catholic Church has evolved considerably since they were written. However valid the particular criticisms of Roman Catholicism were in their own time—and no matter how valid they were, they were as one-sided as most polemics are— they cannot simply be assumed to be valid today. The positive teaching of the documents in the *Book of Confessions* is the crucial matter, and that is what we should pay attention to.

That positive teaching can principally be found in the catechisms, as a part of (or preparation for) the teaching on the Lord's Prayer. Prayer should be a making known of our requests to God (Westminster Larger Catechism, Q. 178; *BC* 7.288), through Christ alone (Second Helvetic Confession XXIII, *BC* 5.218). It can be made in any language, at any time, and in any place, and no language, place, or time is more meritorious than any other (ibid.). Prayer may not be made for the dead (this is a part of the anti–Roman Catholic polemic) or for anything unlawful.

Above all, prayer should follow the Lord's Prayer. The Lord's Prayer is not only a prayer that can and should be learned; it also forms a pattern for all prayer. The three catechisms in the *Book of Confessions* all consider the Lord's Prayer petition by petition.

The Prayer of Prayers

To treat the Lord's Prayer in this way can help us to appreciate anew the meaning of the prayer, and it can give us new insight into what we actually are asking. But it can also obscure the basic movement of the Lord's Prayer through excessive detail. Consequently, it is worthwhile to give some attention to the basic movement of the Lord's Prayer, in order to see how it can be a pattern for all prayer.

The Lord's Prayer is a simple prayer. It's just a series of requests or petitions. Some of those requests encompass the entire universe: "hallowed be thy name; thy kingdom come; thy will be done." Other requests are not so big: "Give us this day our daily bread," "Forgive us our debts," "Lead us not into temptation." In fact, aside from the very beginning ("Our Father who art in heaven") and the very end ("for thine is the kingdom) of the prayer, there is only one thing that is not a request: "as we forgive our debtors." That is the only place in this prayer where we say to God, "You do this, and we'll do that."

A lot is implied in the prayer, of course. To pray for something, if we are not completely hypocritical, commits us. If we pray, "Thy kingdom come," we intimate that we are willing to do our part, whatever it might be, in the coming. If we pray, "Hallowed be thy name," we imply that we ourselves will do our best not to sully that name or take it in vain. There is a commandment about that, after all. And if we pray, "Lead us not into temptation," we hint that if we do encounter temptation, we will do our best to resist it. But only in one place do we say, in effect, "God, you do this and we will do that."

The transition point between the big and the not-so-big requests is in the word *daily*. It comes in the fourth petition: "Give us this day our daily bread." It seems to me that the "daily" carries over: "Forgive us this day our daily debts as we forgive our daily debtors." "Lead us not into temptation this day." "Deliver us this day from evil."

At the end of the prayer, just as at the beginning, things are big. "Thine is the kingdom, and the power, and the glory," isn't just this day; it's eternal. "Our Father who art in heaven" is eternal. God's will is eternal. The kingdom that is coming is wrapped in eternity. We affirm all that in the very act of praying for it. But between the eternity at the beginning of the prayer and the eternity at the end, there is *this day*. This day we will need bread. This day we will need guidance. This day we will need protection. This day we will need forgiveness. And this day we have something to do. This day, suspended between eternities, we have a part to play, and that is to forgive as we have been forgiven.

Here is an outline of how you can work your way through the Lord's Prayer, using it as a pattern for your individual prayers. In each part of the prayer, you will find a focal point for your awareness, and how you might respond to the Lord's Prayer with your own:

Our
Awareness: Others are praying the prayer with me; this is the prayer of the church.
Our prayer is for those who pray this prayer as I pray it, and those for whom we pray.

Father
Awareness: The God who created us loves us and watches over us.
Our prayer is thanksgiving for God's creating and redeeming grace.

Who art in heaven
Awareness: God transcends our world without being absent from us; God both loves and judges the world, and that judgment is the expression of love.

Our prayer is a celebration of love and a welcoming of the judgment that is
   for our benefit.

Hallowed be thy name
Awareness: God is the Holy One.
Our prayer is a way of honoring and respecting God as God (which relates
   to the First and Second Commandments).

Thy kingdom come
Awareness: Our world is beautiful and blessed, but is in rebellion against
   God and shot through with sin.
Our prayer is that God will use us to help make the kingdom actual. Concrete
   ways we can do this are anything in our power that promotes justice,
   extends mercy, eases suffering, or induces joy.

Thy will be done on earth as it is in heaven
Awareness: Doing God's will is the way the kingdom is extended. God's will
   is not arbitrary or erratic; it is the concrete shape of love.
Our prayer is that we ourselves will work to do God's will in the particular
   ways that follow.

Give us this day our daily bread
Awareness: God knows what we need to sustain our lives, and provides for
   us each day.
Our prayer is that this day we truly need . . .

Forgive us our debts
Awareness: We regularly sin against God and others.
Our prayer is that God will forgive us for these particular sins . . .

As we forgive our debtors
Awareness: Forgiveness is our work as Christians.
Our prayer is for grace and mercy for these particular people who have
   wronged us . . .

Lead us not into temptation
Awareness: We are constantly faced with choices that will involve turning
   away from God.
Our prayer is that God will remove these particular temptations from us . . .

Deliver us from evil
Awareness: The evil that is in the world (and in us) is stronger than we are,
   and only God can save us.
Our prayer is that God will act to preserve us and keep us safe from these
   particular evils . . .

For thine is the kingdom, and the power, and the glory forever
Awareness: The end of the prayer returns to its beginning—God.
Our prayer is one of gratitude for all God is and does. We offer all that we
   have and are to the God who gave us all that we have and are.

   To use the Lord's Prayer as a pattern for our prayers is not to simply repeat
the words. It is to follow the logic of the prayer while inserting the details of our
concrete lives into it. We have our particular part in honoring God, advancing

the kingdom, and obeying God's will. This part is unique. No one else can do what we are able to do or be what we are asked to be, simply because no one else will occupy our place in space and time. "Our daily bread," which signifies all that we need to sustain and fulfill our lives, will be different from day to day. The wounds we have received and the wounds we have inflicted will always require acknowledgment and absolution. Our temptations, which will come with monotonous regularity, will always come in different guises. In praying, we can and must be specific about all this. Our prayers will be guided by the Lord's Prayer as a pattern, but they will be uniquely our own.

Without Ceasing

"Pray without ceasing," Paul wrote to the Christians at Thessalonica (1 Thess. 5:17). He did not necessarily mean for them to pray nonstop; he could simply have indicated that they should pray a lot. Prayer sometimes occurs when we pause in our lives, but sometimes we can pray as we go about our lives.

Near Prayers

Many times during an average day, we are very close to prayer. "I'm worried about her," is almost a prayer. "I'm so glad that . . ." is almost a prayer. "Bless his heart!" is, in fact, a prayer, although often we treat it as if it were just an expression. The same is true for many other sayings: "Good heavens!" "I'm so thankful that . . . ," or "It's a miracle!" All that is required to make these near prayers into actual prayers is the awareness of God and the intention to direct these sayings to God. In this way, "I'm worried about her," becomes "Lord, watch over her." "I'm so glad that . . ." is transformed into "Thank you, God." We are often much closer to prayer than we realize. One of the ways to pray without ceasing is to take the step that will turn our near prayers into prayers.

The Prayer of One Word

The single words *God* or *Jesus* are often used as expletives in a form of mild (and increasingly socially acceptable) cursing. This, in fact, is rather close to being a violation of the Third Commandment, but it does not have to be. "God" or "Jesus" can be a simple prayer. It can be a cry for help. It can be a reminder for us that God is present. It can be a curb on undesirable behavior—for example, if we are working on controlling our anger, saying "God" when we feel our temper rising is one way of maintaining our emotional equilibrium. The prayer of one word is as simple as a prayer can be, but it is very much a prayer.

The Prayer of One Sentence

Many people have become familiar with the Jesus Prayer: "Lord Jesus Christ, have mercy on me." This prayer, in one of its several forms, is central to the spirituality of the Eastern Orthodox Church and has attracted much interest elsewhere. It is central to the plot of the stories in J. D. Salinger's *Franny and Zooey*. The Jesus Prayer is somewhat like a mantra in that it is not simply said once but is repeated, often coordinated with one's breathing. Use of the Jesus Prayer is one way of combining Eastern Orthodox and Western spirituality, although theologians of the Eastern tradition often warn that one must have a spiritual guide in order to benefit from this sort of spiritual practice.

One does not have to pray this prayer as a mantra, however. Often, it is exactly the prayer we need in times of trial or stress. The prayer of one sentence, like the prayer of one word, is a perfectly valid prayer and is another way to pray without ceasing. (For a detailed approach to daily prayer that flows from Scripture reading, see appendix B.)

CONFESSION

Confession as a spiritual discipline can be understood in two rather different ways, although the difference is deceptive, for both understandings have a common root. Understood in one sense, confession is an admission of guilt, as in "He confessed that he took the money." The prayer of confession in most Sunday liturgies is confession in this sense; we admit our sinfulness before God and each other and ask for forgiveness. Seen in this way, confession is a kind of prayer, rather than a separate spiritual discipline alongside prayer.

Confession, however, can also be a declaration of belief. The *Book of Confessions* itself uses the word in this sense. All the documents that make up the *Book of Confessions* are statements of the intellectual content of the Reformed understanding of the Christian faith. They are not admissions of guilt (although they discuss sin and guilt rather extensively). Rather, they are declarations of how the church understood its beliefs at a particular time and place. Any individual who says, for example, "I believe that Jesus Christ is the Son of God," is confessing in this sense.

What is the common content of these two understandings of the word *confession*? It is faith. Both the declaration of one's beliefs and the acknowledgment of one's sins require faith, a trust in God that is the ground of all one's action. A confession of faith is not simply a statement about what the church or a given individual believes to be true. It is primarily a statement about where and in whom the church or a given individual has confidence. A confession of sin is not simply a listing of how the church or a given individual has gone astray. It is primarily an honest and sober self-analysis as a response to grace, made in the assurance that there is healing and hope.

Both kinds of confession occur in the Sunday order of worship. The confession of sin precedes the declaration of the word (Scripture and sermon); the confession of faith follows it and is a response to it. It is important to realize that both of these confessions are confessions of the church as such. It is the church that is confessing both its sinfulness and its faith. It is misleading to think of either of these confessions as acts of individuals reciting in unison. On any Sunday, a given individual might or might not have committed some of the sins enumerated in the confession of sin, and might or might not accept the beliefs expressed by the creeds. But the individual's faith and the individual's sin are to be distinguished from the faith or the sin of the church as such. As participants in the life of the church, and therefore as members of the body of Christ, we must take responsibility for both the faith and the sin of the church.

Our individual confessions of faith and of sin flow from the confession of the church. We learned the faith of the church from particular people in particular ways: Sunday school, youth groups, adult study groups, or simple contact with individuals who passed on the faith to us. Even if we learned the faith from books, those books were written by people who were themselves members of the body of Christ. As a spiritual discipline, confessing the faith involves much more than learning, or even assenting to, Christian beliefs. Confessing the faith is thinking the faith, questioning the faith, revising the faith, articulating the faith, teaching the faith, and living the faith in such a way that we are an example and a help to others.

Our individual confessions of sin might be very private moments—indeed, they are quite likely to take place in isolation, for we are almost always deeply ashamed. (If we are not ashamed of that which we are confessing, we are probably not confessing at all.) But they also come from the confession of the church. The liturgical confessions of sin that are used in Sunday worship, such as "Merciful God, we confess that we have sinned against you in thought, word, and deed, by what we have done, and by what we have left undone,"[12] are very general and abstract. They have to be, in order to be applicable to an entire congregation. We as individuals know, however, just what those thoughts, words, and deeds might be. Our individual confessions of sin have little benefit if we stay in the abstract. We must be specific in acknowledging our thoughts, words, and deeds done wrongly or not done at all.

This is not a matter of masochism or self-flagellation. Our confessions of sin are themselves confessions of faith—faith in the grace of God. In confessing, we put ourselves in the hands of the Great Healer, with honesty about who we are and faith in who God is. To move from the stage of purgation to illumination, we must confess our faith and our sin, and we will never be done with this. As the Heidelberg Catechism says, even the holiest of us makes only a small beginning in obedience in this life (Q. 114, *BC* 4.114). But even a small beginning, birthed and nourished by the love of God, is enough.

Making a regular discipline of confession requires both the willingness to examine one's life honestly and a structure to guide that examination. One possible structure is known as the *spiritual examen* or the *examen of conscience* and was suggested by St. Ignatius Loyola in his book *Spiritual Exercises*.[13] Appendix C gives an introduction to the examen and an explanation of how it can be used as part of one's spiritual life.

QUESTIONS FOR COMPREHENSION AND SELF-EXPLORATION

1. This chapter describes three stages of faith: purgation, illumination, and union. What are the characteristics of each?
2. Does this pattern describe your faith journey?
3. This chapter speaks of various kinds of darkness. What has been your experience of darkness? What has sustained you in your times of darkness?
4. How can you pray without ceasing?

5

Love
———

THE PRIORITY OF GOD'S LOVE

"God is love." These words from 1 John are familiar to us—so familiar that we take them for granted. What else would God be? We are no longer surprised by these words, no longer astonished at the reality they represent. The question of whether there actually *is* a God comes up all the time, but we seem to be rather confident that we know what God, if there is a God, is like. The possibility that there is a God and that God is malevolent seems scarcely to occur to us.

It would have been very different when John first wrote that God is love. The people in the empire of ancient Rome believed in many gods, none of them particularly loving. Much of the religion of ancient Rome was concerned not so much with worshiping or serving the gods as it was with appeasing them or escaping their notice. The gods fought with each other, made love to each other (and to various humans), devised traps for each other, grew jealous of each other's followers. Stories were told of unfortunate human beings who became the objects of the gods' wrath, stories that implied it was far better to be overlooked by the gods than to be noticed by them.

Into such a world, the news that there is only one God and that God is a God of love would have been astonishing. The people of ancient Rome had no trouble believing that God, or the gods, existed, but they doubted very much that those gods were good. The sky hung low in the ancient world, as the historian Shirley Jackson Case put it.[1]

For us, the sky has receded. The planets, which once were regarded as divine beings, are now no more than other worlds like our world, although much less habitable. The stars are so far away that even a beam of light takes years (or centuries or millennia) to travel between them. If God is beyond the stars (as God surely must be), then God is impossibly remote for us. And there is hardly any difference between an impossibly remote God and no God at all.

That is the dilemma we face, a dilemma very different from the ancient dilemma. For the ancients, the gods were close but capricious at best and malignant at worst. For us, God is love, but that love seems light-years removed from us. It is easy to love good things, unless they are very far removed from us. Then their goodness becomes irrelevant. The Taj Mahal may well be the world's most beautiful building, but I have never seen it, so it is hard for me to be affected by its beauty. (The fact that I have seen pictures of the Taj Mahal have only made it seem common and clichéd for me, without giving me a sense of its grandeur. I have compared objects and their photographs too often to think that a picture gives anything more than the barest hint of the reality of a thing.) Neither have I seen the *Mona Lisa*, tasted any number of delectable foods, or heard the New York Philharmonic play in Carnegie Hall. Someday, maybe. And if I go outside and look up at the night sky and see only empty space—a cold, lifeless void—it is hard to know what to love.

It is important for us to remember, however, that the same John who wrote that God is love also wrote that we love because God first loved us. In fact, the whole passage is worth recalling:

> In this is love, not that we loved God but that he loved us and sent his Son to be the atoning sacrifice for our sins. Beloved, since God loved us so much, we also ought to love one another. No one has ever seen God; if we love one another, God lives in us, and his love is perfected in us. By this we know that we abide in him and he in us, because he has given us of his Spirit. And we have seen and do testify that the Father has sent his Son as the Savior of the world. God abides in those who confess that Jesus is the Son of God, and they abide in God. So we have known and believe the love that God has for us. God is love, and those who abide in love abide in God, and God abides in them. Love has been perfected among us in this: that we may have boldness on the day of judgment, because as he is, so are we in this world. There is no fear in love, but perfect love casts out fear; for fear has to do with punishment, and whoever fears has not reached perfection in love. We love because he first loved us. (1 John 4:10–19)

John sees Jesus Christ as the supreme expression of God's love. This is fundamental to the Christian faith. But God's love is also seen in the fact that there was a world (the biblical word is *cosmos*) for Jesus Christ to come to. God's love holds the universe in being. All that is continues in existence because God loves it and wills that it continue. Our very lives are the result of God's love. God loved us enough to bring us into being. God loved us enough to give us life—not just life in general, but a particular and unique life, a life that never was before and never will be again. At the moment of our passing, we will see that death itself, which seems to be the cold working of an implacable and impersonal fate, is actually the tender expression of God's love.

Human love is almost always a response to something. We find it very difficult to love on command. But a flower fluttering in a spring breeze, or the wagging tail of a puppy, or a welcoming smile from a complete stranger will inspire love almost instantly in us. Something outside of us, beauty or acceptance or sheer need, summons forth our love. In the case of God, that something is Jesus Christ. Just as he is the truth that summons our faith, he is the love that summons our love. He is the one who comes to us because we cannot go to him.

LOVE IN THE *BOOK OF CONFESSIONS*

While the documents from the sixteenth and seventeenth centuries contain extensive discussions on faith, love is treated much more briefly. This is likely due to the fact that the nature of faith was a matter of much more intensive debate between Protestants and Catholics than the nature of love. Love is encountered as an attribute of God (listed among other attributes), and love as the human response to God is discussed in the context of the first table of the law (the first four of the Ten Commandments).

Love, however—the love of God for the world and human love as the response to God's love—is a prominent theme in the contemporary confessions, the Confession of 1967 and the Brief Statement of Faith.[2] The Confession of 1967 describes the love of God and human love as initiative and response: "The power of God's love in Christ to transform the world discloses that the Redeemer is the Lord and Creator who made all things to serve the purpose of his love" (*BC* 9.15); "God has created man in a personal relationship with himself that man may respond to the love of the Creator" (9.17). This same pattern finds expression in the Brief Statement of Faith:

> In sovereign love God created the world good
> and makes everyone equally in God's image,
> male and female, of every race and people,
> to live as one community.
> (*BC* 10.3, 29–32)

> The Spirit justifies us by grace through faith,
> sets us free to accept ourselves and to love God and neighbor,
> and binds us together with all believers
> in the one body of Christ, the Church.
> (*BC* 10.4, 54–57)

The very purpose of creation, then, was for God's love to find expression, and for this love to be returned by God's creatures. All too often, the Reformed tradition has been interpreted, or perhaps caricatured, as emphasizing God's absolute and arbitrary power, expressed through incomprehensible and irreversible decisions—God as a capricious tyrant. While the power of God is certainly a strong element of Reformed theology, the overall teaching of the *Book of Confessions*, particularly as seen in the light of its last two documents, insists that the sovereignty of God must be understood in terms of divine love, not divine caprice.

THE HUMAN RESPONSE TO GOD'S LOVE

God's love enables our love—but not instantaneously. Humans respond to God's love slowly, haltingly, incompletely, selfishly, and clumsily—just as they tend to respond to the love of other humans. While the capacity to love may be innate, the practice of loving well must be learned over a lifetime.

Are there different kinds of love? It is well known that the Greeks had three different words for love: *eros, philia*, and *agape*. *Eros* is generally understood to be romantic love, *philia* to be friendship or familial love, and *agape* to be disinterested, selfless love.[3] In the New Testament, however, *agape* and its variants is the word used for all forms of love; the word *philia* occurs only once and *eros* not at all. This suggests that it is easy to make too much of the different types of love, and that all forms of human loving have something profound in common. Every form of human love that genuinely is love has some element of selflessness and some element of selfishness, whether that love be the love of comrades, family members, sexual partners, or humanity in general. Even the purest human love is never entirely pure, and even the love most tainted by lust and possessiveness will on some level desire the good of the other.

Still, there must be some difference between loving God and loving a friend, a spouse, or a child. If it is true that "those who do not love a brother or sister whom they have seen, cannot love God whom they have not seen" (1 John 4:20b), there is still a gulf between that which is seen and that which is not—a gulf that is rather difficult to cross. We humans experience the love of God through the created order. If it is true that we love because God first loved us and that if we do not love our neighbor whom we have seen we cannot love God whom we have not seen, then we must learn to respond to God's love by loving our brothers and sisters. All love is ultimately from God, but we experience that love through intermediaries: parents and family, the gifts of the earth, the care of a congregation. Likewise, by learning to love those intermediaries, we learn to love God.

LOVE GROWS UP

On Loving God by the twelfth-century saint Bernard of Clairvaux is a remarkable treatise from the Middle Ages that describes the steps we go through in learning to love God.[4] (If you have read Thomas Merton to any great extent, you will recognize the name of Bernard. Merton refers to him again and again, especially in the diaries and journals.)

Bernard holds that there are four stages in our learning to love God, which are not like steps on a ladder but more like points on a circle:

> Love of oneself for the sake of oneself
> Love of God for the sake of oneself
> Love of God for the sake of God
> Love of oneself for the sake of God

The first step is self-love; Bernard thinks that we all start here. A legitimate, healthy self-love is a mark of a normal human being and is probably necessary for our happiness—and even our survival. Our own selves are precious to us, and they should be. They are precious to God too. We want to care for ourselves. We want to achieve our goals. We want to live life in a way that contributes to the goodness of things. We want to own the things that give us happiness or pleasure.

There is also, of course, a sort of self-loathing that goes along with this love of oneself for the sake of oneself. Oftentimes we don't like ourselves very much. We doubt our worth, our attractiveness, our acceptability. A chance remark or a simple frown can evoke shame and doubt in us almost as quickly (or perhaps more quickly) than a smile can evoke love and happiness. We may not be our own severest critics, but we are probably our most neurotic ones. Our self-criticism and self-loathing is probably not based on the reality of ourselves or the way other people actually feel about us. I've known many people who have reached middle age without coming to terms with their high school experiences. The point is that it might take some work, some introspection, and possibly some therapy for us even to get to the stage where we can love ourselves for the sake of ourselves. Just getting to the starting gate might be hard enough.

There is nothing at all wrong with self-love, provided that one does not stop there. A self-love that can *only* love oneself is pathological. True self-love does not remain with the self. So much of our life depends on our relationships with others that the welfare of those others inevitably becomes our concern. We care about our families and our friends because our lives are woven together. So our love of the self for the self's sake expands to others. It also, in Bernard's view, expands to God.

Sooner or later, Bernard writes, we are bound to become aware that our lives are dependent on the work of God. The one who sends rain on the just and the unjust also sends rain on the crops, and the sunshine as well. If all good things come from God, as the Bible tells us, then our relationship with God is central to our well-being. This discovery, that God's goodness and our happiness are related to each other, marks the transition into Bernard's second stage: the love of God for the sake of oneself.

Our entering the second stage depends on our perception of God's goodness. This is what connects our faith and our love: Our growth in faith (described in the purgative and illuminative stages of spiritual development) leads to growth in love—provided we can respond to love with love. Especially, our understanding of Jesus Christ as one who is *for us* must lead to our own self-understanding as people who are, or at least can be, *for others*. In this development, we are well on our way to the third and fourth stages of love.

Unfortunately, all too many preachers and churches stop at the second stage and never move again. They turn the gospel message into the single theme "What God can do for you." This can be on the rather crass level of the "God wants you to be rich" school of televangelism, to the more rarified promise of spiritual happiness, internal peace, or a place in heaven. Whatever the enticements (some of which, I hasten to say, are entirely biblically justified), the basic promise is the same: You should love God because God can do good things for you.

There is nothing at all wrong with this second stage, but it is like the first: it becomes pathological if one cannot move through this stage to the next. We move from regarding God as a means of satisfying our needs to regarding God as supremely good, true, and lovely. We learn to love God for God's own sake. We learn to love God because God is lovable.

This can take a while. Appreciation of God's goodness surely goes hand-in-hand with the purgative task of weaning ourselves from our inordinate attachments to the things of the world. For most of us, that task never ends. But we do begin to get a glimmer along the way of what Jesus meant in talking about the pearl of great price, for which one was gladly willing to exchange everything.

As we grow in our love of God, the component of our self-interest will diminish. We will seek to do God's will without thought of reward or favor. This is not only in order to please God. Rather, as we grow in our love of God, we will also grow in our love of God's work. We will learn to love the world the way that God loves the world: with pity and compassion and patience. We will learn to look on others as our brothers and sisters, united in Christ. Secure in God's love, we will become more capable of *agape*, because we will stop seeking or needing a response from the world.

This all sounds rather idealistic and otherworldly in a society shot through with road rage, winning through intimidation, power lunches, power ties, and power wardrobes. Perhaps it is. But it seems to me from my study of the history of Christianity that Christians have been most effective when they have been idealistic and otherworldly, and most likely to betray their Lord when they have joined in all the power games. The fact that most of us will spend a good part of our Christian lives hovering on the border between stages 2 and 3 does not at all mean that stage 3 is unattainable. It only means that the way to stage 3 is marked by patience, prayer, and (above all) the presence of the Spirit.

One would think that Bernard would leave it at that, but there is a fourth stage: the love of oneself for the sake of God. We are back to loving ourselves, but in a new way. The characteristic of this stage is that we truly understand that we are children of God: loved, sanctified, and redeemed. "See what love the Father has given us, that we should be called children of God; and that is what we are" (1 John 3:1), wrote John. What would our lives be if we could truly accept this—if we could simply accept God's love as a fact and stop trying to earn or deserve it? The basis of our self-love would then not be our worth or our need or our achievement, but only God's love. We would not only love because God first loved us, but we would love *ourselves* because God first loved us. In so doing, we would become vessels of God's love for the world.

Bernard thought that few people got to this stage during their lifetimes. It seemed to him more likely to be a characteristic of life in heaven rather than life on earth. I am sure that I have not attained it; I am not even sure I understand it.

But I have caught this glimmer. I am the father of a grown son. I love him dearly—sometimes I am surprised at how much—and I have loved him that way since before he was born. There have been many times when he was disappointed with himself, or frustrated with himself, or ashamed of himself. During most of those times, I wasn't disappointed or frustrated with him, or ashamed of him. Some of the times when he wasn't happy with himself I was rather proud of him. There were only a few times when I was very disappointed and angry with him; more often than not, he had trouble understanding why. During all those times, I wished he could see himself as I saw him. I wished he could understand his growing up the way I did.

I think God looks at us like that. I think God often wishes that we could see ourselves with his eyes, so that we could understand why it was that he was proud of us when we were most disappointed and angry at us when we were at our most proud. If we could really learn to see ourselves that way, we might get some idea of what this last stage is all about.

Those are the four stages of Bernard's understanding of love. Knowing God is crucial; it is in knowing God more and more fully that we move from one stage to the next. Here again we have a circle, for if our knowing God better means that we love God more, it is also true that our loving God more leads to our knowing God better. In some ways, it's like getting onto a merry-go-round: we have to jump and hang on. It is some comfort to know that there are hands to catch us.

Is there a relationship between the stages of faith discussed in the last chapter (purgation, illumination, union) and these stages of love? They are not really identical, but they might well be inseparable.

It would be a mistake to understand the stages of faith as a solitary quest to be one with God. Faith in God necessarily commits one to participating in God's work. Jesus' words to Peter, "Do you love me? Feed my sheep!" are addressed to every Christian (John 21:15–17). The stages of faith are more than the progressive knowledge of God. They are also steps in the convalescence of the soul. They mark the diminishment of one's slavery to sin and self, and consequently the freeing of one to enter into the life of God and the freeing of one to give oneself to others in the service of God. So also, the stages of love mark the diminishment of one's self-centered concern, and consequently the freeing of one to love God—and not God only, but all that God loves. It might be possible to love others without loving God (as the famous poem by Leigh Hunt "Abou Ben Adhem" suggests), but it is not really possible to love God without loving others. "Those who say, 'I love God,' and hate their brothers or sisters, are liars; for those who do not love a brother or sister whom they have seen, cannot love God whom they have not seen" (1 John 4:20). To choose for God is necessarily to choose for others, and to choose against others is to choose against God.

Accordingly, the spiritual maturation marked by either the stages of faith or the stages of love is never a matter of leaving the world in order to become closer to God. Rather, it is a matter of learning to be in the world in a different way. Faith and love are not so much ideas or emotions as they are an orientation—a fundamental openness toward our neighbors that is enabled by God's loving power.

THE DISCIPLINES OF LOVE

Listening and Speaking

In the previous chapter, we examined Scripture reading and prayer as listening and speaking to God—the fundamental disciplines of faith. Listening and speaking to others are also disciplines. They are among the disciplines of love. Loving our neighbors must be done in the concrete. It is not enough—in fact, it is not anything—to love our neighbors in general without any interaction with this particular neighbor, here and now.

True dialogue is a discipline and an art. It has to be learned and practiced. It is astonishing how many of our conversations with other people are not dialogues at all. Instead, they are alternating monologues. I say something and then have to pause and catch my breath, during which time the other person says something else. I wait until the other pauses, then I jump back in and continue where I left off.

We have all been in conversations like that, and we have all been frustrated by them. Doubtless our conversation partners were also frustrated. It is aggravating to speak and be misunderstood; it is even more aggravating to speak and not even be heard.

We have to learn to listen to each other in such a way that we can put the other's thoughts into words the other will recognize. Pastors will doubtless remember seminary exercises in "reflective listening"—that is, being able to summarize another's comment accurately and without intrusive emotional overtones. It was occasionally embarrassing for me when I was sure I had understood someone correctly and reflected that person's conversation accurately, only to be told, "No, that isn't what I meant at all."

To truly listen to a person is one of the most precious gifts we can give. We don't have to solve people's problems (even if we could) or restore order to their tangled lives. Just being heard can make a vast difference in someone's outlook. Listening is truly a gift of love, an *agape* gift.

There is a corresponding discipline we must also practice, and that is speaking. We have to learn to speak with patience and precision so that we will be understood—and we must realize that there are times when we will be misunderstood, no matter how much patience and precision we employ. Human communication is never 100 percent efficient. There is always some gap in understanding, even between people who know each other very well. We should not be offended or insulted if we have to repeat ourselves or rephrase an idea. Jesus did not hesitate to repeat himself. The Old Testament is full of God's repetitions—warnings and promises over and over again. Helping someone to understand us is a gift of love, just as much as is working to understand another.

The upshot is that true dialogue is a discipline—a spiritual discipline. It is a discipline of love, for it overcomes the separation between people and breaks through the misunderstandings that can often lead to anger, prejudice, and even violence. Dialogue is a demanding discipline, to be sure. Once we really start to practice it, we become aware of how often we miss each other in our conversations. But we can practice that discipline every day.

Worship and Sabbath

We can listen to and speak to all that we love: other people, animals, plants, even the planets and stars. What "speaking" and "listening" varies, of course, according to who or what we are listening and speaking to. But worship is reserved for God alone.

To worship is to acknowledge God as God. That is the sole fundamental. Beyond that, there is tremendous variation: worship can be corporate or solitary, indoors or outdoors, vocal or silent, sung or spoken, early in the morning or late at night. If God is acknowledged as God, worship is truly worship. If God is not acknowledged as God, whatever is happening is simply some form of entertainment or delusion.

Worship is thus an orientation before it is an activity. It is the willingness to acknowledge God as God. Whatever form that willingness might take, from an explicit desire for God to a vague sense that there must be something more, worship does not happen if it is not there.

Accordingly, when a religious community gathers at a scheduled time in order to express and strengthen the faith of its adherents, that is more an opportunity for worship than it is worship as such. For some of those gathered, this opportunity might result in a life-changing encounter with the living God. For others, it might be just an hour or two spent in a rather benign boredom, with no appreciable effect on their lives.

Worship as a spiritual discipline is not so much an endless succession of life-changing events as it is an availing oneself of those opportunities in which worship might happen. In short, it involves going to church. It involves going to church whether or not one feels like it, gets anything out of it, puts anything into it, or learns anything from it. It involves going to church as an expression of love for God and God's people, without consideration of some psychological or spiritual reward or benefit.

In the Reformed tradition, the stress has been on worship as an encounter with God through the word. The Westminster Confession describes worship in this way:

> The reading of the Scriptures with godly fear; the sound preaching, and conscionable hearing of the Word, in obedience unto God with understanding, faith, and reverence; singing of psalms with grace in the heart; as, also, the due administration and worthy receiving of the sacraments instituted by Christ; are all parts of the ordinary religious worship of God. (BC 6.116)

All these activities, including the sacraments, are ways in which we meet God through the word of God. The proper response to this encounter is not so much adoration or contemplation, although those are never absent, as it is obedience.[5]

Hearing and responding to the word of God is also, of course, the dynamic we encountered in Scripture reading and prayer. The difference here is that in worship we hear and respond to the word of God as a community rather than as solitary individuals. This is what gives worship its dimension as a discipline of love. Obedience to the will of God *is* love: "They who have my commandments and keep them are those who love me; and those who love me will be loved by my Father, and I will love them and reveal myself to them" (John 14:21). This love is not love for God rather than all else; it is love for God that extends to all else.

The progression of the stages of love we just examined can be applied directly to worship. One can begin regular worship for the sake of oneself (or for any number of other reasons), grow into worship for God's sake, and develop a sense that one participates in worship not only for God's sake but for the sake of the worshiping community.

This is not automatic or instantaneous. One Sunday, we might be in worship full of love for God and God's people, while the next Sunday, we might sit in church seething with resentment at how meaningless our worship seems. Our attitudes about worship and our response to worship vary as widely as our attitudes and responses to anything else. The crucial factor is being there, much more so than our feelings *about* being there.

The Confession of 1967 describes the double movement of a congregation: "The church gathers to praise God. . . . The church disperses to serve God" (*BC* 9.36–9.37). While these movements are distinct, they are as inseparable as breathing in and breathing out. The praise of God in the sanctuary and the service of God in the world inform, strengthen, and support each other. The service of God without the praise of God is shallow and ineffectual; the praise of God without the service of God is an empty sham.

Consequently, it is wrong to see Sunday worship as a sixty-minute religious interruption in a fundamentally secular existence—a time-out for God, as it were. Instead, Sunday worship and weekly service are twin components of a life lived in the presence of God, which acknowledges God as God. In this sense, worship is continual in both the gathering and the dispersion. Worship only ceases when the acknowledgment of God ceases. In short, when worship stops, hell begins.

The gathering of the congregation for corporate worship is not one spiritual discipline among others. It incorporates all spiritual disciplines: hearing the word and praying in response to the word; confessing and renewing; speaking and listening; giving and receiving; hoping and planning. Spiritual practices, whether or not they take place on an individual level or in isolation, have their roots in the life of the body of Christ, the church, before God. The disciplined spiritual life does not really add practices to Sunday worship. Instead, it extends the practices that are already there.

To understand worship as acknowledging God as God means that the first four of the Ten Commandments apply directly to worship. We think of the Fourth Commandment, "Remember the sabbath day, and keep it holy," as being the commandment that applies to worship. But the three commandments that precede it—"You shall have no other gods before me," "You shall not make for yourself an idol," and "You shall not make wrongful use of the name of the Lord your God," all specify what it means to acknowledge God as God.[6] The Sabbath commandment, in the Reformed understanding, is about the context for worship: the particular time when the community gathers to worship together.

Many of the creeds and catechisms in the *Book of Confessions* deal with worship and the Sabbath day, particularly Westminster and the Reformation-era documents. They reflect their polemical context in that they attack Roman Catholicism. It is important, however, to understand what they are upholding as much as what they are criticizing.

Giving and Stewardship

A particular moment in most worship services, at least in the United States, is when wooden or metal plates are passed through the congregation as a way of collecting money. This offering, as it has come to be called, has its roots in the early church. Scripture was read and expounded, then the elements of communion were brought forward to be consecrated and served. After the service, the elements were taken to those not able to attend.[7] In this way, the elements that symbolized Jesus' body and blood in the service, and thus the redemption promised in the gospel, went into the world. The offering, the giving of the church—whether internal or external—was a response to the gospel. The good news enables sharing. It enables generosity. God's goodness, both in a spiritual and a material sense, is to be shared.

Currency and checks are more abstract than bread and wine. It is easy for us to lose track of what we give, even in our own congregations. Money sent to some other part of the nation or to some other corner of the world through an intermediary such as a denominational or international mission organization starts to seem very abstract indeed. We lose sight of the fact that we are helping others, because we never see those others face-to-face.

Three realizations lie behind the practice of giving: (1) we have neighbors in need, (2) we have enough to share, and (3) we are agents of God's love.

Many religious traditions base their understanding of the necessity of giving on a fourth realization: the importance of devaluing the material in favor of the spiritual, and the subduing of the body in favor of the spirit. Ascetic practices of self-deprivation and even self-punishment are endorsed in order to "subdue the flesh."

The Reformed tradition has never been entirely happy with this fourth realization. While it certainly has stressed moderation and self-control, it never has gone so far as to endorse a kind of masochism as a spiritual discipline or to endorse poverty as a superior form of life. John Calvin broke with the entire medieval tradition, which considered usury to be one of the seven deadly sins, in supporting the lending of money at interest.[8] Acquiring money and property was seen as a form of industry blessed by God, provided one realized that providing for neighbors in need was a required duty of Christians and that one's property was held in a kind of trust to meet the needs of the neighbor. In the words of the Heidelberg Catechism on the topic of the Eighth Commandment ("You shall not steal"):

Q. But what does God require of you in this commandment?

A. That I work for the good of my neighbor wherever I can and may, deal with him as I would have others deal with me, and do my work well so that I may be able to help the poor in their need. (BC 4.111)

In the understanding of the confessions, then, it is a form of stealing to refuse to work for the good of our neighbors or to withhold our goods from the poor.

Consequently, the spiritual discipline of giving and stewardship requires a certain amount of honest discernment. Some of our material resources are necessary to maintain our lives and the lives of those who depend on us. Some of our resources are set aside in order to safeguard our futures. Some of our resources are doubtless devoted to comfort, convenience, and pleasure rather than sheer survival. Some of our resources are to be shared. How much?

In part, this discernment depends on knowing the difference between what we need and what we want—especially as we are quite likely to perceive a want as a need. In part, this discernment must rest on trust in God. To hoard all we have in order to safeguard our futures against every conceivable circumstance is a form of practical atheism, as much a mockery of God as justifying spending all we have while saying, "God will provide." Neither unabashed hedonism nor tightfisted miserliness is a form of faith, and certainly neither are forms of love. Instead, faith and love are characterized by "glad and generous hearts" (Acts 2:46).

Giving and stewardship are enacted prayers. They are our response to God's love made tangible through our sharing with others. They force us to make decisions about what we truly need, what we can do without, and what we can share in the name of love. "It is more blessed to give than to receive," Jesus said (Acts 20:35), but we can give only because we have received already. Therefore, we are called to share.

QUESTIONS FOR COMPREHENSION
AND SELF-EXPLORATION

1. Is there a difference between self-love and self-obsession? What kind of self-love is legitimate? What kind of self-love is destructive or evil?
2. What does the phrase "God is love" mean to you?
3. Do Bernard of Clairvaux's stages of love reflect your own experience?
4. How would you like to grow in love?

6

Hope

HOPE FORMED BY FAITH AND LOVE

Faith, hope, and love are not different things. They are the same thing, seen in different ways. Hope is the temporal aspect of love. Hope is love facing the future. Hope is also the temporal aspect of faith. Hope is faith that God is at work in ways that are not yet apparent. Faith and love, working through time, result in hope.

Christian hope is not sheer optimism or trust in one's luck. Still less is it based on the expectation of spiritual salvation or material reward for belief or meritorious works. Neither is it the inevitable result of scientific discovery, technological progress, or social evolution. Christian hope is grounded only in the presence and activity of God in history.

This points to a further paradox in the Christian faith: God is active in time but is not bound by or subject to time. Time is a feature of the created order—perhaps *the* feature of the created order—and all creation is subject to it. The Creator is not. But the Creator is not removed from time either. The story the Bible tells is the story of the eternal God working in the temporal world.

Paul discusses this in the eighth chapter of the book of Romans:

> For the creation waits with eager longing for the revealing of the children of God; for the creation was subjected to futility, not of its own will but by the will of the one who subjected it, in hope that the creation itself will be set free from its bondage to decay and will obtain the freedom of the glory of the children of God. We know that the whole creation has been groaning in labor pains until now; and not only the creation, but we ourselves, who have the first fruits of the

Spirit, groan inwardly while we wait for adoption, the redemption of
our bodies. For in hope we were saved. Now hope that is seen is not
hope. For who hopes for what is seen? But if we hope for what we do
not see, we wait for it with patience. (Rom. 8:19–25)

The creation's "bondage to decay" has been put in a new light by the world-
view of modern science. The current scientific model, presented in popular
form in dozens of books and television shows, holds that the universe had
a beginning—the "big bang"—and that it will have some kind of an end.[1]
Understandings of what this end might be like vary widely, but anything
human will end with it, if it has not ended long before.

The story of the Bible and this scientific theory agree in the bare fact that
the universe had a beginning. The scientific theory suggests that the universe
will have an ending, while the Bible holds that it will have a new beginning
that is entirely the work of God. The true distinctiveness of the biblical view,
however, does not lie with the beginning and ending of the universe. The distinctiveness of the biblical view is its position that the center of the history of
the universe—the supremely important, crucial event between the beginning
and the ending (or new beginning)—is the appearance of an itinerant teacher
in the Roman province of Judea who was the Son of God enfleshed.

The appearance of Jesus Christ compounds the paradox of time and eternity. In the saga of the people of Israel, we see the eternal God acting in
time. In the history of Jesus of Nazareth, we see God *existing* in time. Every
document in the *Book of Confessions*, and perhaps every work of Christian theology ever written, struggles to somehow articulate this paradox. No matter
what, the phrases of the Nicene Creed (and their equivalents in the other
constituents of the *Book of Confessions*) "eternally begotten of the Father" and
"crucified under Pontius Pilate" stand in tension with each other, each making the other almost incomprehensible. Consistently in the church, however,
every attempt to dissolve the paradox, by eliminating either the eternity or the
temporality of Christ, has been condemned as a heresy. The biblical witness
testifies to both, and therein lies our hope.

Christian hope lies both within history and beyond it. Within history,
there is God's promise: a promise of a people who will bless the earth (Gen.
12:3), of a liberator for the captives (Exod. 3:7–10), of return from exile (Isa.
43:5–7), of the birth of a savior (Matt. 1:21), of the savior's return (Acts 1:11),
and of the remaking of creation (Rev. 21:1).[2] Beyond history, there is resurrection as a triumph over death (1 Cor. 15:12–15), a final judgment (Rom.
2:6–8), and eternity with God (John 14:1–3). The Christian understanding of
hope, and the spiritual characteristics that spring from it, must take account
of both the within and the beyond.

HOPE BEYOND HISTORY

"We who must die demand a miracle," W. H. Auden wrote.[3] This miracle, the resurrection of Jesus, has been at the heart of the Christian faith from the beginning. It is not just an odd fact or a seemingly improbable occurrence. It is, according to the New Testament, the ground for our hope: In the earliest document of the New Testament, Paul wrote, "For since we believe that Jesus died and rose again, even so, through Jesus, God will bring with him those who have died" (1 Thess. 4:14). The resurrection of Jesus was, for Paul, the central teaching of the Christian faith: "If Christ has not been raised, then our proclamation has been in vain and your faith has been in vain" (1 Cor. 15:14).

Jesus' own teaching, as presented in the New Testament, is complex. In the Gospel of John, much of what Jesus says is about himself. In Matthew, Mark, and Luke—the so-called Synoptic Gospels—Jesus speaks of the kingdom of God that is coming. The church inherited both of these strains of teaching, combining them into a hope that looks to the return of the resurrected Christ as the realization of the kingdom of God. This can be seen in the Nicene Creed:

> On the third day he rose again
> in accordance with the Scriptures;
> he ascended into heaven
> and is seated at the right hand of the Father.
> He will come again in glory to judge the living and the dead,
> and his kingdom will have no end.
> . . . .
> We look for the resurrection of the dead,
> and the life of the world to come. Amen.
>
> (BC 1.2, 1.3)

These two themes—resurrection of the dead and the coming of the king-dom of God—are not irreconcilable, but they do stand in some tension with each other. Emphasizing one to the exclusion of the other has consistently created problems for the church. Emphasizing resurrection to the exclusion of the kingdom has led to a spirituality of individual salvation, in which the Christian task has been understood to be remaining faithful to Christ while enduring the world until death opens the door to heaven. The world itself is understood to be full of evil and temptation, to be resisted and ultimately abandoned without being redeemed or transformed. Emphasizing the king-dom to the exclusion of resurrection has resulted in either an apocalyptic mentality, in which Christians withdraw from the world to wait for the end, or an identification of the kingdom of God with earthly political entities, in which a kingdom or nation is regarded as divine in and of itself. Christian hope must be both within history and beyond it if it is to be authentic. Within history, Christian hope is centered on justice and reconciliation. Beyond history, Christian hope is centered on reconciliation and eternal life.

In the book of Genesis, death is the punishment for Adam's sin: "By the sweat of your face you shall eat bread until you return to the ground, for out of it you were taken; you are dust, and to dust you shall return" (Gen. 3:19). This is repeated in the New Testament, in Paul's juxtaposition of Christ and Adam: "Therefore, just as sin came into the world through one man, and death came through sin, and so death spread to all because all have sinned. . . . For if the many died through the one man's trespass, much more surely have the grace of God and the free gift in the grace of the one man, Jesus Christ, abounded for the many" (Rom. 5:12–15). In the hands of St. Augustine, this passage became the proof text for the idea of original sin, although Augustine drew back from the universalist theme implied by Paul.

In the *Book of Confessions* we do find the theme that death is the divinely ordained punishment for sin (Scots Confession, *BC* 3.02–3.03: "And thus everlasting death has had, and shall have, power and dominion over all who have not been, are not, or shall not be reborn from above.") The death of Christ, however, changes things. Death is no longer a punishment; it is a transition: "Our death is not a reparation for our sins, but only a dying to sin and an entering into eternal life" (Heidelberg Catechism, *BC* 4.042).

The New Testament has this view of the intertwined course of history and the individual's destiny: The Christ who died on a cross and was buried in a tomb rose from the dead in bodily form. He ascended into heaven but will return at the conclusion of a time of violent strife. At his return, the dead will rise. Christ's coming will bring a new creation, a New Jerusalem, in which there will be no death, sorrow, or pain. Individuals will be judged and assigned either to this new creation or to a place of torment. At this judgment, Christ will stand in the place of those who accepted and followed him, and his righteousness will substitute for theirs.[4]

The authors of the documents in the *Book of Confessions* knew this biblical picture very well and struggled to take account of it when they treated death, resurrection, and the end of history. But they also had a view of the human person inherited from Greek philosophy (specifically Plato and his followers) that was in some tension with it. In this view, humans are composed of two parts: a mortal, vulnerable body, and a naturally immortal, preexistent soul. At death, the soul is released and only the body perishes.

The Hebrew and Greek words that are often translated as "soul" in the Bible have a complex range of meanings. They do not tend to signify a naturally immortal substance encased in a body. They can mean life, or breath, or mind.[5] When the New Testament speaks about life after death, it speaks in terms of resurrection of the body rather than immortality of the soul.[6] Resurrection of the body is a miracle of God.

The Reformers knew that the Bible spoke of resurrection of the body, but they firmly believed that human persons had souls that were naturally immortal. Consequently, they put the concepts together and came up with a two-stage understanding of life after death: Upon death, the souls of the elect went immediately to God, while the souls of the reprobate went immediately to hell. At the second coming of Jesus, bodies were resurrected, reunited with their souls, judged, and then dispatched either to the heaven or the hell where their souls had been residing.[7]

This process seems unnecessarily complicated, perhaps an indication that a conceptual difficulty had not been solved so much as ignored. While the language of *body* and *soul* may be useful in order to distinguish between that which dies and that which lives, it tends to drive a wedge into something that is a fundamental unity: the human person.[8] It also tends to treat life after death as a natural process rather than a divine miracle. The Confession of 1967, in its brief discussion, avoids this language entirely and states simply, "Life in Christ is life eternal" (*BC* 9.26). The God who gives life is stronger than death. The resurrection of Jesus Christ is not simply an event in the past; it is a promise for the future.

In the Reformed understanding of Christian spirituality, death is neither to be courted nor feared. It is not to be feared because even death cannot separate us from God, and it will not triumph over God. At the point of death, we humans are helpless. We can no longer work or think or feel or do anything else on our own behalf. We are, in fact, dead. But we are also enfolded within the might and mystery of our divine maker, who is full of love and who has promised not to abandon us or cast us off. In death, God's grace is all we have. But God's grace is enough, and we need not fear.

Death is not to be courted, however. We must not wait passively for death. God has given us life for a purpose. The church, and the individuals within it, have been given a commission.

On Election

Historically, the Reformed tradition has been identified with the doctrine of double predestination: the teaching that God, before creation, determined who should be saved (the elect) and who should be damned (the reprobate) without regard to any merit or foreseen or foreknown good works. In the Westminster Confession of Faith, this is known as the "eternal decrees."[9]

The early Reformed theologians felt that they had good biblical ground for this teaching. They were also convinced that the matter at stake was the sheer gratuity of grace: No human merit, cooperation, or even desire affected or influenced the divine decision. To say anything else, they thought, was to make grace a reward for some kind of human achievement, rather than the gift of God. Furthermore, since our election is grounded in God's will rather than human achievement, we need not fear that it can somehow be lost or jeopardized. We can concentrate on obedience to God's will out of gratitude rather than attempting to somehow earn our salvation.

To contemporary ears, the doctrine of double predestination sounds bizarre. It seems monstrous for God to condemn souls to eternal punishment out of "the unsearchable counsel of his own will," as the Westminster Confession puts it (*BC* 6.020). Rather than unmerited grace, modern Christians (Reformed or not) tend to see this doctrine as teaching undeserved punishment, and they find it baffling.

In fact, this is one of the instances in which the *Book of Confessions* records a dramatic shift in Reformed thinking. The "Declaratory Statement" added to the *Westminster Confession* in 1903 says

> that the doctrine of God's eternal decree is held in harmony with the doctrine of his love to all mankind, his gift of his Son to be the propitiation for the sins of the whole world, and his readiness to bestow his saving grace on all who seek it; that concerning those who perish, the doctrine of God's eternal decree is held in harmony with the doctrine that God desires not the death of any sinner, but has provided in Christ a salvation sufficient for all, adapted to all, and freely offered in the gospel to all; that men are fully responsible for their treatment of God's gracious offer; that his decree hinders no man from accepting that offer; and that no man is condemned except on the ground of his sin. (*BC* 6.92)

Some have seen this "Declaratory Statement" as a welcome modification and a return to more biblical language; others have regarded it as a betrayal. Whether this statement can actually be harmonized with the language of the original document seems rather problematic, but it certainly represents a movement away from the conceptual scheme of Westminster.[10]

From the point of view of Reformed spirituality, however, the importance of the doctrine of election remains: God's grace is not simply a possibility. It is an actuality. It is the foundation of the spiritual life, from which we live, and its trustworthiness depends on the power and presence of God rather than on any human effort or achievement. The proper response to grace is, as the Heidelberg Catechism stresses, to offer ourselves "as a living sacrifice of gratitude" (*BC* 4.032).

The result of this is to take the stress of the spiritual life off of any single human experience—such as a conversion, sacrament, or faith decision—and put it squarely on obedience as grateful response throughout the whole of life. It makes very little sense, from the Reformed perspective, to speak of being "saved" at any particular point in life. The most that can be said is that at some particular point (perhaps many particular points) we become aware of the grace of God that had been operating throughout our life.

This grace did not wait on our acceptance or approval. It was and is sovereign. We might have received it as the world received the Christ child, unnoticed in the night; we might have wrestled with it as did Jacob and been wounded in the wrestling; we might have been engulfed by it, as was Jonah; we might have been vanquished by it, as was Paul. There are as many patterns as there are people, but the result is the same: grace triumphant, gratitude obedient.

As we have seen, such obedience is not a mindless following of particular directives. Rather, it involves the highest degree of human creativity, intelligence, and initiative. It is doing particular things, to be sure, but above all it involves being in the world in a particular way. This is the link between God's election and the Christian's vocation. Election entails vocation—hence the *Book of Order*'s insistence that one of the great themes of the Reformed tradition is "the election of the people of God for service as well as for salvation" (*BO* F-2.05).

HOPE WITHIN HISTORY

The Bible is as much about the activity of God *within* history as it is about that which lies *beyond* history. This is, in fact, one of the central claims of the Bible. God acts throughout history, by means of particular events, particular peoples, and particular individuals:

> In everlasting love,
> the God of Abraham and Sarah chose a covenant people
> to bless all families of the earth.
> Hearing their cry,
> God delivered the children of Israel
> from the house of bondage.
> Loving us still,
> God makes us heirs with Christ of the covenant.
>   (*BC* 10.3)

These lines, together with much of the rest of the Brief Statement of Faith, are in some sense a summary of the history recounted by the Bible. The themes of covenant and deliverance, which pervade the Old Testament, are extended into the New, which sees their culmination and completion in Jesus

Christ, and their extension in the mission of the church. The Bible tells the story of the work of God from the creation of the world to its remaking, and the confessions testify to that story.

The Providence of God

One of the most pervasive themes in the *Book of Confessions* is that all things are determined by God's will. This is a middle position between two extremes: that all things happen by pure chance and that all things happen because of a mindless fate. In rejecting both randomness and impersonal or mechanical determinism, the confessions teach that God's will is the decisive factor in all that happens. The Second Helvetic Confession puts it this way: "We believe that all things in heaven and on earth, and in all creatures, are preserved and governed by the providence of this wise, eternal and almighty God" (*BC* 5.029). This universal governance, according to the Heidelberg Catechism, is the basis of our trust:

> Q. 26. What do you believe when you say: "I believe in God the Father Almighty, Maker of heaven and earth"?
>
> A. That the eternal Father of our Lord Jesus Christ, who out of nothing created heaven and earth with all that is in them, who also upholds and governs them by his eternal counsel and providence, is for the sake of Christ his Son my God and my Father. I trust in him so completely that I have no doubt that he will provide me with all things necessary for body and soul. Moreover, whatever evil he sends upon me in this troubled life he will turn to my good, for he is able to do it, being almighty God, and is determined to do it, being a faithful Father. (*BC* 4.026)

It is important to realize what this affirmation does and does not say. It certainly is not a guarantee of happiness or material prosperity or the absence of trouble in the Christian life. Neither does it posit a system of rewards and punishments for good and bad behavior. Any such thinking is absolutely foreign to the Reformed tradition. All the confessions acknowledge that human beings will have difficulties in their lives. There is no moral calculus that explains these difficulties or enables us to avoid them. But throughout, God is working for our good and the good of all.

If this is the case, why is there pain and suffering? Why do catastrophes and natural disasters occur? Why do evil people seem to be allowed such free reign without divine intervention? These and similar questions constitute one of the most persistent and perplexing issues in all Christian theology. Known as *theodicy*, it is the attempt to understand how it can be that God is supremely good and supremely powerful while there still is evil in the world.[11]

Both the discussion and its history are long and complicated. However, the church has clung to certain basic affirmations:

> Creation is good. The material world is good. Matter as such is not evil, and matter as such is not the problem. The first chapter of the book of Genesis is God's blessing upon the entire created order.
>
> God might allow evil for reasons that are mysterious, but God does not will evil, nor did God create evil.[12]
>
> God's ultimate purpose in the drama of redemption is to overcome and eliminate evil.
>
> The church is one of God's instruments in carrying out this purpose.

Consequently, the church's task is more to oppose evil than to comprehend why evil might be; it certainly is not to comprehend why evil might be without opposing it. Furthermore, the opposition to evil must be carried out in a particular way: through championing and upholding the good. Especially, according to the Confession of 1967, the church's special task (and the special task of the individual Christians who constitute the church) is to be an agent of reconciliation: "This community, the church universal, is entrusted with God's message of reconciliation and shares his labor of healing the enmities which separate men from God and from each other" (*BC* 9.31).

The church has often construed the task of Christian spirituality to be to control and subdue the material: our passions, our "lower nature," our physical drives and urges. Moderation became abstinence, chastity became virginity, and self-control became self-abuse. As a result, the spiritual life became conceived as a kind of war between one component of the self against another, and the triumph of the one involved the repudiation or extermination of the other. One can see elements of this viewpoint in the *Book of Confessions*, such as these two passages from the Scots Confession and the Westminster Confession

> For as soon as the Spirit of the Lord Jesus, whom God's chosen children receive by true faith, takes possession of the heart of any man, so soon does he regenerate and renew him, so that he begins to hate what before he loved, and to love what he hated before. Thence comes that continual battle which is between the flesh and the Spirit in God's children, while the flesh and the natural man, being corrupt, lust for things pleasant and delightful to themselves, are envious in adversity and proud in prosperity, and every moment prone and ready to offend the majesty of God. (*BC* 3.13)

> This sanctification is throughout in the whole man, yet imperfect in this life: there abideth still some remnants of corruption in every part, whence ariseth a continual and irreconcilable war, the flesh lusting against the Spirit, and the Spirit against the flesh. (*BC* 6.076)

Much of contemporary spirituality tries to avoid dividing the human person into component parts that struggle against each other. Rather, it tries to speak holistically, seeing the human person as a unity living a life shaped by the grace of God. This does not eliminate struggle, but it relocates it. The Confession of 1967 reflects that

> the new life does not release a man from conflict with unbelief, pride, lust, fear. He still has to struggle with disheartening difficulties and problems. Nevertheless, as he matures in love and faithfulness in his life with Christ, he lives in freedom and good cheer, bearing witness on good days and evil days, confident that the new life is pleasing to God and helpful to others. (*BC* 9.23)

The task of the Christian life, then, using terminology of the Confession of 1967, is both to witness to and to facilitate reconciliation, and the demeanor of the Christian is freedom and good cheer. Reformed Christians are not the gloomy, self-obsessed, inwardly conflicted neurotics that the caricatures of Calvinism suggest. They are people who live in a hope based on the invincibility of the grace of God.

VARIETIES OF HOPE

In earlier chapters, we discussed stages of the development of faith and of love. There are no corresponding stages of hope in the Christian tradition. Nevertheless, one can distinguish between various kinds of hope. Here we will look at three: hope for, hope that, and hope in.

Hope for has to do with desire. There are many things for which we might hope. Some of them are tangible: a good meal, a new car, a good return on investments. Some are not: we might hope for love, for friendship, for peace of mind. Either way, *hoping for* has to do with what we lack and what we want.

There are two pitfalls: hoping for the wrong things and hoping in the wrong way. Sometimes we hope for things that will hurt us, either because they are damaging in and of themselves or because pursuing them diverts us from that which we ought to be doing. It is easy to start believing that some particular object will satisfy us or make us happy, when it will not. The experience of the Preacher of Ecclesiastes is the experience of many: "Then I considered all that my hands had done and the toil I had spent in doing it, and again, all was vanity and a chasing after wind" (Eccl. 2:11).

But even those things that we legitimately need and can appropriately hope for can trap us, for we can desire them too much. There is much truth in the fundamental Buddhist insight that craving leads to suffering. It is the same truth that is articulated in the Westminster Shorter Catechism's treatment of the Tenth Commandment: "The Tenth Commandment forbiddeth all discontentment with our own estate, envying or grieving at the good of our neighbor, and all inordinate motions and affections to anything that is his" (*BC* 7.081).

Modern American society is wedded to the idea that individuals can change their "estates"—their stations and conditions in life. We have constantly been taught that desire, intelligence, and appropriate preparation (the right education at the right school, or at least the right degree from the right school) will enable us to better our lives. Given this, the admonition to be content with our own estate sounds almost bizarre. What is the point of living if it is not to build a better life for ourselves and our children? Isn't "Be content" another way of saying, "Be lazy"?

However, the Bible warns over and over that "a better life" is not to be measured by more things. "Do not store up for yourselves treasures on earth, where moth and rust consume and where thieves break in and steal" (Matt. 6:19), Jesus tells his followers. The book of James puts it even more bluntly: "You want something and do not have it; so you commit murder. And you covet something and cannot obtain it; so you engage in disputes and conflicts" (Jas. 4:2). However much we might want or need something, our hope cannot rest there without imperiling our souls. *Hoping for* has its limits.

Hoping that has to do with situations. We hope for things or qualities that we feel we lack; we hope that something happens to change our lives for the better: "I hope that I get over this cold." "I hope that I get a raise." "I hope that I meet someone special." Such hopes are not always on our own behalf. Often, they have to do with others: "I hope that she finds a job soon." "I hope that his operation is successful." "I hope that our church finds a new pastor before Christmas." Such hopes are among the near prayers discussed earlier: they are one step away from being prayers of intercession. They become prayers when we turn them over to God.

Our aspirations, dreams, and intercessions are—or can be—just as legitimate as our desires for certain things. Aspirations and dreams reflect the future we envision for ourselves, and intercessions reflect the future we envision for others. To envision the future is part of what makes us human. Because we can imagine how things might be, we can direct our efforts to bringing that to reality. This is what shapes our lives.

There is a danger here, however, just as there is a danger in our desire for the things that we lack. If we become too enamored with our own vision of what might be, we lose sight of other possibilities. We can be fixated on our own dreams to the extent that they form controlling obsessions and threaten to become idols. Finally, they can displace our willingness to submit ourselves to the will of God or to consider the possibility that the future we envision might not be the future God intends. Even our highest hopes and best dreams for the future of all—world peace, an end to poverty and illness, a willingness to live without wasting the resources of the earth—can become idolatrous if they lead us to monomaniacal clinging to our own vision rather than to humble dedication to the divine purpose. Sometimes we must trust in the future we do not see, and hope for possibilities we cannot envision or even articulate. "Hope that is seen is not hope," wrote Paul. "For who hopes for what is seen?" (Rom. 8:24).

This leads us to the third kind of hope. If *hoping for* has to do with the things we need or desire, and *hoping that* has to do with the future we envision, *hoping in* has to do with persons. Specifically in our context, it has to do with God. This kind of hope is our response to the providence of God.

It is perfectly possible, of course, to hope in persons other than God. To say, "I have hope in her," is very similar to saying, "I have faith in her." We might say this about a political leader, or about our children, or about a physician or a teacher. It is an expression of confidence—not necessarily that the person in question will do this or that particular thing, but that the person will act in a particular way. A doctor would fulfill our hope not by performing this or that operation, but by using all his training and skill to bring about healing. A child would fulfill our hope by becoming a responsible and productive adult. *Hoping in* is much less specific than *hoping for* or *hoping that*.

To hope in God, then, is more than hoping God will bring about a particular situation or grant us a particular thing. It is trusting that God is present and active in all situations and in everything that comes our way, whether or not we apprehend or understand that presence and activity. It is this expression of trust that is the foundation for the Brief Statement of Faith and that is expressed consistently in the Heidelberg Catechism—the trust that is at the heart of Reformed spirituality.

The danger here is quiescence. To say that God is constantly at work is not at all to say that human work in the service of God is pointless, superfluous, or unnecessary. Rather, it is the constancy of God's work that makes such human work possible and productive.

THE CALLING OF A CHRISTIAN

In the story that the Bible tells, calling is a constant. God calls individuals and whole peoples to be messengers and coworkers in the task of redemption. Noah is called to build an ark. Abram is called to go to a new place and establish a people. Moses is called to lead the enslaved people back to their homeland. Prophets are called to declare God's word. Disciples are called to accompany Jesus during his lifetime and to carry on his work after his resurrection.

There are certain constants to these call stories. The first is that the initiative is entirely God's. God's command to Abram, "Go from your country and your kindred and your father's house to the land that I will show you" (Gen. 12:1), comes without any preparation at all. Moses had no hint that the burning bush would be the summons that would shape his life. God said to Jeremiah, "Before I formed you in the womb I knew you, and before you were born I consecrated you; I appointed you a prophet to the nations" (Jer. 1:5). The disciples whom Jesus called were simply going about their daily tasks when the summons came.

A second feature of calls is that people were called to a task. The calls were not simply a blessing or an indication of divine favor; they were a summons to duty. Abraham was to go to a new land. Moses was to be the deliverer of his people. Isaiah was to tell the people words they would refuse to hear. The disciples were to be fishers of people. In short, people were called to very specific tasks in God's service, and God worked through them to accomplish his purposes.

A third feature is the promise that God would accompany those whom he called. "I will be with you," God said to Moses (Exod. 3:12). "Do not say, 'I am only a boy'; for you shall go to all to whom I send you, and you shall speak whatever I command you. Do not be afraid of them, for I am with you to deliver you," God told Jeremiah (Jer. 1:7–8). The disciples received Jesus' assurance: "Remember, I am with you always, to the end of the age" (Matt. 28:20).

A fourth feature of the calls is that they usually involved hardship and suffering. Moses led the Israelites through a forty-year wandering in the desert before bringing them to the border of the promised land. Jeremiah was rejected and vilified, and finally thrown into a well to perish. He ended his life in exile in Egypt. Zechariah was stoned to death in the courtyard of the temple. Peter was said to have been crucified upside down at his own request, believing himself unworthy to die in the way that his Lord had died. And this is Paul's summation of his life as an apostle:

> Five times I have received from the Jews the forty lashes minus one. Three times I was beaten with rods. Once I received a stoning. Three times I was shipwrecked; for a night and a day I was adrift at sea; on frequent journeys, in danger from rivers, danger from bandits, danger from my own people, danger from Gentiles, danger in the city, danger in the wilderness, danger at sea, danger from false brothers and sisters; in toil and hardship, through many a sleepless night, hungry and thirsty, often without food, cold and naked. (2 Cor. 11:24–27)

Jesus was not exaggerating when he told his followers, "As for yourselves, beware; for they will hand you over to councils; and you will be beaten in synagogues; and you will stand before governors and kings because of me, as a testimony to them" (Mark 13:9). The people in the Bible were not called to a life of prosperity, ease, or worldly honors. They were called to be faithful, to endure, to persevere, and to cling to the Lord no matter what happened.

The later church was fond, perhaps overly fond, of telling the stories of the martyrs and dwelling on the gruesome details of their sufferings. They were heroes, models of fidelity in spite of enduring instances of savage torture and suffering agonizing deaths. The Bible takes a somewhat different tack; it tells of their shortcomings and failures as much as of their triumphs. Samson blabs out the secret of his strength. David commits deliberate murder in order to hide his adultery. Elijah despairs. Jonah runs away. Judas betrays. Peter denies.

Peter is the emblematic disciple, both in his victories and his failures. He gyrates from bravado to cowardice, from confession to timidity. He is, in short, human. Jesus takes this humanity into account. In Luke's version of the Last Supper, he says, "Simon, Simon, listen! Satan has demanded to sift all of you like wheat, but I have prayed for you that your own faith may not fail; and you, when once you have turned back, strengthen your brothers" (Luke 22:31–32). Peter has the opportunity not only to try again but to make his own failure a source of strength for those around him.

God's work continues, and God's way of working continues. God has not ceased to call human beings. We might wish for something as explicit as the people in the Bible got: the clear voice of God, or Jesus motioning to us and saying, "Come." Our calls tend to be more elusive than that. We have seen that discovering where we fit can be a long and frustrating enterprise, with many false starts and blind alleys. Nevertheless, all the features of the biblical calls apply to us: God takes the initiative, we are called to particular tasks, God does not abandon us in the doing of those tasks, and we will likely encounter difficulties and trials. Furthermore, we will fail—perhaps not in the way that Peter failed, but we will surely fail. And we will be given the chance to receive forgiveness, rededicate ourselves, and turn our failures into sources of strength.

Our tasks will be unique, for we are unique. Each of us lives at a particular time, in a particular place, with particular abilities and resources. Each of us, therefore, will have opportunities to do what no one else can do. But each of us will find these opportunities in the context of the universal task of all Christians: the work of reconciliation.

Reconciliation is the theme of the Confession of 1967. It proclaims, "God's reconciling work in Jesus Christ and the mission of reconciliation to which he has called his church are the heart of the gospel in any age" (BC 9.06). This reconciliation is the work of hope. In one of the seminal passages of the New

Testament, Paul writes, "So if anyone is in Christ, there is a new creation: everything old has passed away; see, everything has become new! All this is from God, who reconciled us to himself through Christ, and has given us the ministry of reconciliation" (2 Cor. 5:17–18). The "us" here is universal: it is the entire body of Christ, and every individual member of that body. Each of those individual members, each unique person, has unique opportunities to work toward reconciliation. This overarching task of the church assumes countless different forms, as Christians find themselves in countless different situations. The fundamental goal, however, remains the same: to help bring about peace between humans and God, and between humans and each other, that is not simply the absence of hostility but is the presence of love.

DISCIPLINES OF HOPE

The disciplines of hope spring from our faith that God is at work at all times, whether or not we perceive or comprehend that work. They also shape the human work by which we participate in God's work, the work we do as a matter of obedient freedom. These works have to do with caring and equipping. In Christian hope, we both embrace and shape the future. In this light, we will discuss custodianship, patience and planning, and reconciling.

Custodianship

A custodian is a guardian. Custodians have things or people in their care and are responsible for the protection, safety, and well-being of them. Of course, the custodianship of people is very different from the custodianship of things, and there are different kinds of custodianship of people according to the different kinds of human relationships. We will consider the custodianship of things, the custodianship of life, and the custodianship of children.

Custodianship of Things

Our relationship to things is one of the central themes of our lives. There are things we own. There are things we want. There are things we use. There are things we avoid because they are potentially dangerous or unpleasant. In the discussion of *hoping for*, we looked at the dangers of desire and the potential for idolatry inherent in things. Custodianship has to do with using things for the right purposes in the right way, and using no more than we need.

A part of Christians' self-examination asks this question: What do I own and why? Some of the things we own are required for our physical survival, such as clothing, food, and shelter. Some of the things we own contribute beauty or joy to our lives; a painting, a musical instrument, or a flower garden can give us pleasure and delight in human creativity and God's good world that makes such creativity possible. But some of the things we own can control our lives, and our ownership of them can turn into a kind of slavery. This slavery to things was what led Henry David Thoreau to write in his classic, *Walden*, "The mass of men lead lives of quiet desperation," and to see how much he could do without.[13]

Thoreau had his predecessors, of course. One of them was St. Benedict of Nursia, the founder of the Benedictine Order and author of its Rule, both of which are still very much with us. One of the ideals of that order, and of the entire monastic movement, was poverty: the attempt to live without personal ownership of anything, in imitation of Christ.[14]

It is easy to romanticize poverty unless one has actually experienced it. The Bible is constantly concerned about alleviating the plight of the poor and is constantly critical of those who have and do not share. As we have seen, passages in the *Book of Confessions* consider it a form of stealing to withhold needed goods from one's neighbor. There are, however, spiritual issues with regard to things (acquiring, owning, using, and disposing thereof) that are not tied to the needs of our neighbors.

With regard to the disciplines of hope, our evaluation of our relationship to things is as much negative as positive. It is a question of attitude: In my day-to-day living, am I giving as much importance to things as I am to God? If the answer is not a quick and decisive "No!" we need to realize that those things have become idols to us, and we should divorce ourselves from them. Such things are not evil in and of themselves any more than the wood or gold that makes a physical idol are evil in and of themselves. But we put them to an evil use when we give them the kind of power over us that only belongs to God.

Custodianship of Life

There is a difference between a thing and a living thing, even those living things we claim to own, such as pets or working animals or even plants. Life creates obligations. We can destroy or dispose of inanimate things in ways that we cannot or should not with regard to living things. I can smash a dish, and all I have to do is clean it up. But I can go to jail for smashing a dog or a cat in the same way.

The Bible is absolutely clear that all life is God's gift and never ceases to be God's gift. The charge of Genesis 1:28, "Be fruitful and multiply, and fill the earth and subdue it; and have dominion over the fish of the sea and over the birds of the air and over every living thing that moves upon the earth," does not give any kind of license for cruelty or heedless destruction. Rather, it is an assignment of responsibility. The earth is the Lord's, and remains so.[15]

Furthermore, God's work of redemption in Jesus Christ includes the entire creation: "For the creation waits with eager longing for the revealing of the children of God; for the creation was subjected to futility, not of its own will but by the will of the one who subjected it, in hope that the creation itself will be set free from its bondage to decay and will obtain the freedom of the glory of the children of God" (Rom. 8:19–21). Our caring for the living things of creation is a spiritual duty. We must seek the welfare of the other and of all living things, as well as our own welfare.

Custodianship of Children

We must certainly seek the welfare of children—all children, not just our own offspring. Jesus singled them out, not only as those who are his own, but also as examples for us: "Whoever does not receive the kingdom of God as a little child will never enter it" (Mark 10:15).

The Reformed tradition has constantly held that the children of believing parents are included in God's covenant.[16] This is the justification for infant baptism in Reformed churches. It also implies a special obligation in those churches to provide instruction and example for those children whom it baptizes. If living the faith is difficult, transmitting the faith compounds the difficulty. Anyone who has ever taught Sunday school, sponsored a youth group, or led a catechism class knows that special rigors are involved. But the results can be remarkable. Almost all adult Christians can point to Sunday school teachers or youth leaders who taught, guided, and inspired them.

To bear, raise, and teach children is the very expression of hope, both for the children themselves and the world we bequeath to them. Ideally, this hope is both to make the world better for our children and to raise children who will better the world. Realistically, parents often fear both for their children and their children's world. Indeed, some give the conditions of the world (in the present or the envisioned—and feared—future) as a reason for refraining from having children.

Nevertheless, the *Book of Confessions* presents Christian marriage as an instrument of sanctification and spiritual growth for the partners who enter it, and the family as both the result of and the expression of God's reconciliation. The Westminster Confession, in a chapter rewritten by both the Presbyterian Church in the United States and the United Presbyterian Church in the United States of America, describes marriage as "established and sanctified for the happiness and welfare of mankind," in which the partners live together "cherishing a mutual esteem and love, bearing with each other's infirmities and weaknesses, comforting each other in trouble, providing in honesty and industry for each other and for their household, praying for each other, and living together the length of their days as heirs of the grace of life" (*BC* 6.131). The

Confession of 1967, in keeping with its overarching theme, describes marriage in terms of reconciliation: "Reconciled to God, each person has joy in and respect for his own humanity and that of other persons; a man and woman are enabled to marry, to commit themselves to a mutually shared life, and to respond to each other in sensitive and lifelong concern; parents receive the grace to care for children in love and to nurture their individuality" (BC 9.47).

In the Reformed understanding, marriage in some sense replaces the monastery as the context of spiritual development. The partners who enter into marriage do so through promises: vows that express how they intend to live their lives. Spiritual maturation occurs simply in the process of living together, as the partners grow and change, wound and forgive, enjoy triumphs and contend with failures. The partners have a priestly responsibility to each other and to their children in leading the family in prayer, praying with and for all the family members, admonishing and correcting each other, and simply loving each other. Thus, the family grows spiritually.

Of course, things do not always turn out this way. Many families separate when the partners divorce. Often the children become a kind of rope in a tug-of-war as parents struggle over visitation, custody, and upbringing. Or sometimes the opposite happens, and one or both parents seem to act as if they had divorced the children as well as their partner. Whatever reconciliation might occur after divorce is often hard won and partial at best.

The nature of the spiritual life, however, is that any sort of progress is often partial and hard won. We are sinful beings who live in a sinful world, and our lives are much more characterized by the cycle of falling short, repenting, and trying again than by continual success and improvement. In every difficult situation—and certainly in the dissolution of a marriage, which is one of the most difficult situations people ever face—there are opportunities for renewal, creativity, and hope. Divorce, however painful, does not have to be a disaster for children. Custodianship, in the form of gentle and responsible guidance and love, can continue to work to bring children to maturity and committed faith.

Patience and Planning

Patience and planning are disciplines related to *hoping that*. In some sense they are reciprocal: planning involves doing, and patience involves waiting. But the reciprocity is not contradiction; rather, it is the rhythm that reflects our understanding of the relationship between God's work and our share in God's work.

In his letter to the Romans, Paul links patience and hope: "If we hope for what we do not see, we wait for it with patience" (Rom. 8:25). He lists patience as one of the fruits of the Spirit (Gal. 5:22). In the New Testament, patience is not only an attribute of the saints but also an attribute of God (Rom. 2:4). God is patient with us; therefore, we must be patient with each other.

This patience rests on faith and trust. The affirmation that begins the Brief Statement of Faith, "In life and in death, we belong to God" (*BC* 10.1), is the grounding of patience as a mark of the Christian life. This is not sheer optimism, the belief that sooner or later everything will be all right. Neither is it a denial of the difficulties and pain involved in living. Indeed, in the New Testament, patience and endurance are often linked, as in the letter to the Colossians: "May you be made strong with all the strength that comes from his glorious power, and may you be prepared to endure everything with patience, while joyfully giving thanks to the Father, who has enabled you to share in the inheritance of the saints in the light" (Col. 1:11–12). We may hope that things will turn out in a certain way, and it is perfectly legitimate to pray that they do. If they do not, though, patience is called for: patience, endurance, and hope, coupled with the knowledge that God is working in and through all the events of our lives.

This is entirely different from quiescence: simply doing nothing because "God is in charge." God is indeed in charge, but God has chosen to invite human beings to share in the work of redemption.

In the third chapter of Genesis, human labor is put under a curse: "Cursed is the ground because of you; in toil you shall eat of it all the days of your life; thorns and thistles it shall bring forth for you; and you shall eat the plants of the field. By the sweat of your face you shall eat bread until you return to the ground, for out of it you were taken; you are dust, and to dust you shall return" (Gen. 3:17–19). This curse, however, is not work as such, for even in the garden people had work to do (Gen. 2:15). Rather, the curse is work that is unproductive: daily toil that results only in thorns and thistles. A redeemed world contains the possibility of redeemed work—work that will truly be a blessing to the earth and its people, work that can and does accomplish something: "Man is free to seek his life within the purpose of God: to develop and protect the resources of nature for the common welfare, to work for justice and peace in society, and in other ways to use his creative powers for the fulfillment of human life" (*BC* 9.17).

Such work requires intelligence, planning, industry, and persistence. It is not the opposite of patience; indeed, such work requires patience. It is not quick, and it is not easy. People can and do devote their entire lives to accomplishing one tiny piece of the great work of redemption: one step that increases our capacity for healing, sharing, comforting, or renewing the created order. And that one step matters. It is part of the slow but inexorable advancement of the kingdom of God, the kingdom that is measured by mustard seeds and grains of wheat and pinches of salt.

To plan, to work, and to have patience, then, are the disciplines that are tied to *hoping that*. They are disciplines not so much in the sense of repetitive activities as persistent attitudes. As such, they can be rather fragile, for our attitudes are affected by many things: our moods, our surroundings, the state of our bodies, a change in the weather. A part of the patience we must have is patience with our own selves, to not let discouragement and depression undermine our commitment and our hope. No matter how much or how little we accomplish, in a day or a week or a lifetime (and we are very poor judges of the worth or extent of our accomplishments), our hope is not in ourselves, our capacities, or our deeds. Our hope is in God alone, whose strength strengthens our strength and whose hands guide our hands. *Hope for* and *hope that* must rest on *hope in*.

Reconciling

In the creation story that begins the book of Genesis, God proceeds through differentiation. Light is separated from darkness, sky from land, water from earth. In this way, the initial chaos was brought to order. But differentiation makes conflict possible. The first death recorded in the Bible was a murder— and a fratricide. Six generations after Cain killed Abel, Cain's descendant Lamech boasted to his wives, "I have killed a man for wounding me, a young man for striking me" (Gen. 4:23). The story the Bible tells is that sin, once in the world, burgeoned. One act of disobedience became a perpetual state of disobedience; one murder became wholesale slaughter; one garden became numerous battlefields; brothers became enemies; worship became idolatry. The result was a world alienated from God and divided against itself, a world in need of a reconciliation it was incapable of accomplishing on its own.

The Confession of 1967 describes reconciliation as the great work of God, the work we are called to share: "God's reconciling work in Jesus Christ and the mission of reconciliation to which he has called his church are the heart of the gospel in any age" (*BC* 9.06). This assertion is based on a firm biblical warrant: "All this is from God, who reconciled us to himself through Christ, and has given us the ministry of reconciliation" (1 Cor. 5:18).

The reconciliation the Bible envisions involves the entire cosmos. It is more than peace between God and individuals, or God and whole peoples, or individuals or whole peoples with each other. In Romans, Paul speaks of a creation set free from bondage (Rom. 8:19–21), and in 1 Corinthians of a creation fully united in God (1 Cor. 15:28).

The last chapters of the book of Revelation speak in a similar, highly visual and symbolic way, of a new heaven and a new earth, in which death, mourning, crying, and pain are no more (Rev. 21:4). This is the ultimate hope: a cosmos fully at peace, united by love.

We are, of course, far from that point. In some sense, we seem to be further than we have ever been. The technological advancement of humanity, in which we put so much hope, seems to have given us the capacity to threaten all life on earth, either by weapons of war or the wasteful and destructive by-products of manufacturing and industry. A few decades ago, we wondered whether human life, or any life, could survive the effects of nuclear war. We now wonder if human life, or any life, can survive the effects of global warming. The twentieth century, which some christened the "Christian century" at its inception, ended with multiple wars, acts of (in part) religiously motivated terrorism, an increasingly secular mentality in many cultures, and the so-called mainline denominations wondering if they could survive. Given all this, many wonder if the hope of reconciliation is simply an illusion.

Reconciliation with God

This questioning of the possibility of reconciliation might seem new in light of the optimism of the last few decades, in which expectations of progress and better living were tied to technological development, economic growth, and the seemingly endless supply of natural resources. But for much of its history, Christianity understood itself to be living in a world that was crumbling. Jesus spoke of a terrible time, which he apparently understood to be imminent (Mark 13:30). The entire New Testament reflects this expectation, and the book of Revelation gives it an extended, and rather gruesome, exposition. The persecution of the early church, the dissolution of the Roman Empire and the barbarian invasions, the recurring waves of bubonic plague and other diseases, and the constant threat of war all suggested to Christians that the end was near. Reconciliation with God seemed to be an urgent necessity, and it seemed to entail repudiation of the world. The rise of monasticism in the early church gave an institutional form to such repudiation.

The churches of the Reformation embraced life, but they still carried on a polemic against "the world": "Hence, we are enlisted in the holy military service of Christ that all our life long we should fight against the world, Satan, and our own flesh" (BC 5.189). Reconciliation with God, in their view, committed them to a lifelong struggle that was in part a struggle with the values of the world around them (in spite of the fact that the world was ostensibly Christian) and in part a struggle with their own internal temptations and lusts.

There is no doubt that reconciliation with God involves a struggle, but it is important to locate that struggle precisely. The reconciliation itself is a fact. It is Jesus' work, and it is done. But the appropriation of that reconciliation is a life-long task. Paul is constantly reminding his readers that who they are in relation to God has changed, so who they are in relation to the world and to others must change. He asks, "How can we who died to sin go on living in it?" (Rom. 6:2).

Of course, on one level, it is perfectly possible to go on living it, as the confessions stress: "I am still ever prone to all that is evil," says the Heidelberg Catechism (Q. 60, *BC* 4.060), and the Westminster Larger Catechism delivers this indictment: "No man is able, either of himself, or by any grace received in this life, perfectly to keep the Commandments of God, but doth daily break them in thought, word, and deed" (Q. 149, *BC* 7.259). Our struggle is in large part tied to this "daily"—our persistent failure to live as those who have been reconciled to God. However, Heidelberg reminds us that it is the very fact of this reconciliation that enables us to struggle at all: "God, without any merit of my own, out of pure grace, grants me the benefits of the perfect expiation of Christ, imputing to me his righteousness and holiness as if I had never committed a single sin or had ever been sinful, having fulfilled myself all the obedience which Christ has carried out for me, if only I accept such favor with a trusting heart" (Q. 60, *BC* 4.060). Our struggle, in short, is not a struggle to become acceptable or reconciled to God; it is a struggle to become who and what, in the eyes of God, we already are.

We have seen two accounts of the development of the Christian life: the three stages of faith (purgation, illumination, and union) and the four steps of the ladder of love (love of self for the self's sake, love of God for the self's sake, love of God for God's sake, love of the self for God's sake). Both of these are descriptions of this central struggle to become who we already are. The various disciplines associated with faith and love help us to carry on in this struggle with faith and hope. To live each day being the one God has declared me to be is to live as one who has been reconciled to God. It is to live with our hope lodged in God and nowhere else.

The Ministry of Reconciliation

We have seen many times in this study that to move away from the world in order to become closer to God will, sooner or later, take us back to the world. This is so because God is constantly moving toward the world. God is not static, motionless, or uncaring. God goes forth into the world: through creation itself (which is an ongoing activity, not a one-time event), through the incarnation of the Son, through the sending of the Spirit. To be united with God is to share in God's going forth. To love oneself for God's sake is to love all that God loves. To hope in God is to dedicate oneself to the future that God is bringing about.

The last chapter of the Gospel of John tells the story of the resurrected Jesus meeting his disciples at the Sea of Galilee. They had spent the night fishing, with no success ("Apart from me you can do nothing"; John 15:5). As the sun rose, they saw Jesus on the shore, and suddenly their nets were full. Peter dove into the water and swam ashore, leaving the rest of the disciples to haul in the nets and land the boat.

After breakfast, Jesus asked Peter, "Simon, son of John, do you love me more than these?" (John 21:15). He repeated this question three times—once for each of Peter's denials. Each time, Peter said that, yes, he did love Jesus. Each time, Jesus responded with a command: "Feed my lambs." "Tend my sheep." "Feed my sheep."

In a sense, Jesus was recommissioning Peter. Peter was called, and his denials did not invalidate the call. Jesus was not going to let Peter go back to living as a fisherman; the sheep needed tending. If Peter truly loved Jesus— and there is no reason to deny that he did—Peter was going to have to care for those Jesus loved.

So it is with all Christians. If we truly love Jesus, if we truly love God, our love will not be a warrant to turn away from God's world. The demands of spiritual growth might take us out of the world for a time, but that time is only for growth, refreshment, and renewal. We will always find our spiritual life leading us back to the place where we feed the lambs and tend the sheep. As the Confession of 1967 puts it, "To be reconciled to God is to be sent into the world as his reconciling community" (BC 9.31).

How each Christian does this is as unique as each Christian. One's service as an agent of reconciliation is shaped by one's talents, resources, and place in the world. There is no superior or inferior, there is no better or worse, there is no religious or nonreligious in this work of reconciliation. There are only the opportunities that each person's life provides to testify, soothe, heal, forgive, and renew in the name of the Lord Jesus Christ. Some might do this through a ministry of prayer; some might do this through a ministry in the healing arts; some might do this through study and teaching; some might do this in community, even cloistered community; some might do this through times of extended solitude; some might do this by working for the welfare of the impoverished or dispossessed; some might do this simply by responding to the needs of their neighbors. This is the point at which the ministry of reconciliation becomes a spiritual discipline: when one is always willing to do what one can with what one has as an expression of one's love of God. Thus, and only thus, do we follow the God who goes forth.

All this is true to the Reformed understanding that "Love the Lord" sum-marizes the first table of the law and is the essence of spirituality, while "Love your neighbor" summarizes the second table of the law and is the expression of spirituality. Jesus' question and subsequent command to Peter—"Do you love me? Feed my sheep"—summarize the law. The embodiment of grace, the one who is grace itself, gave grace the shape of law—law as the guiding principle of life. This understanding of the spiritual life is the treasure that is carried in the earthen vessel of the Reformed tradition. It is not the treasure that is ours alone. It is the treasure that all Christians share when they are most truly who they strive to be.

QUESTIONS FOR COMPREHENSION AND SELF-EXPLORATION

1. How are death and hope related to each other?
2. Is election just about going to heaven?
3. What do you hope for in life? How have your hopes changed as you have matured?
4. What are your hopes for the world? How are you working to make those hopes a reality? Do you see God working in the world to bring about those hopes? If so, how?

Appendix A

Bible Study as a Spiritual Discipline

A Practical Guide

APPROACHING SCRIPTURE

The first step in reading Scripture as a spiritual discipline is to find a reading plan. It is tempting (and also daunting) to try to read the Bible just as one would read other books: by starting at the beginning and reading through to the end. Many people have tried this and succeeded, but many others have become confused and bored upon encountering chapter after chapter of genealogical material or legal statutes that seemed archaic and even barbaric.

The Bible is not a single book; it is a library of books. The fact that we encounter the Bible as if it were a single book, with its pages sewn together and bound in a single hard cover, tends to make us treat the Bible as if it were a book rather than a collection of books. To simply read the Bible from beginning to end is something like reading all the books in one's local library in the order that they are shelved, starting at the front door and ending at the fire exit.

There are many other ways of reading the Bible.[1] One can proceed chronologically, following the history of Israel and the church; one can investigate certain topics, such as faith or miracles; one can explore certain literary forms, such as poems, parables, or law codes. All of these are legitimate ways of engaging in Bible study.

A lectionary is a list of Bible readings. Sometimes such a list is tied to the worship of the church. Many churches use the Revised Common Lectionary to determine the Scripture readings Sunday by Sunday.[2] Other lectionaries are designed to provide a reading plan for individuals. Such a lectionary can be found in the *Book of Common Worship*.[3] It provides daily Scripture readings over a two-year period. Following this plan, you will read through most of the Old Testament during the two years. You will read the New Testament twice. Here is a way to begin:

How to Prepare

1. Find a quiet, comfortable place where you are not likely to be interrupted.
2. Turn off the television, radio, stereo, and telephone.
3. Have your Bible, your reading plan, a notebook or journal, and a pen or pencil with you.

How to Begin

1. Relax. Quiet your mind by listening to your breathing. Center your attention on the God who loves you. You might think of something that symbolizes God for you: a candle, a dove, a kind and gentle parent. If you find your mind turning to other matters, refocus on your symbol. Some people find that saying a single word, such as "Jesus" or "grace" or "Spirit" helps them to center their attention.
2. Say a brief prayer. Ask God to reveal God's self through the Scriptures.

The Discipline

1. Do the reading. If something about the text puzzles you, write the question down and go on. Don't get up to do research—that can wait.
2. In your journal, write down any words or phrases that capture your attention or stimulate your imagination.
3. If you feel that God is speaking to you in a special way, write that down in your journal.

How to Conclude

1. Thank God for any new insights that have come to you.
2. Ask God for what you need for the rest of the day—whatever that may be.
3. If you have any special items of thanksgiving or intercession, jot them down in your journal.
4. End with the Lord's Prayer.

What You Can Expect

1. The Scriptures are God's living voice to you. You can expect that something about the text will speak to your personal situation.
2. Expect God to work slowly. You may be shaped or changed in ways you do not realize until later. Have patience and trust in God.
3. As you persevere, you can expect your desire to read the Bible to grow stronger. At times, however, you may experience dry spells when this does not happen. This is the point to seek out a spiritual friend and discuss the situation.

Pitfalls

1. It is easy to procrastinate and postpone, but try to keep to a schedule. Let the habit of the discipline become established in you.

2. Sometimes you must change your schedule. Don't worry about that. Do your reading when you can. But don't confuse an interruption with an emergency.

3. If you have expectations that are not being fulfilled, it may become difficult to let God lead. If you are experiencing disappointment, frustration, boredom, or feelings of abandonment, write about this in your journal and/or discuss it with a spiritual friend.

4. Become aware of what in your life obstructs or prevents this discipline. Things like strong anger, temptation, feelings of shame and guilt, and feelings of spiritual superiority are very destructive to your Bible-reading discipline. The way to handle these problems is to recognize them and pray through them, asking God for help. "Lord, help me read" is a perfectly valid prayer.

Appendix B

Disciplined Prayer

A Practical Guide

APPROACHING PRAYER

The discipline of prayer reflects the discipline of reading Scripture. In fact, the discipline of prayer is a response to the discipline of reading Scripture. If Scripture is the way God normally speaks to us, prayer is the way we normally speak to God. Prayer as a discipline involves making prayer a regular part of one's life. The following model builds on the approach to Scripture outlined in appendix A.

How to Prepare

1. Find a regular time or times during the day when you can devote yourself to prayer. Morning, midday, and evening prayer is a common pattern, although two or even one time of prayer might be more comfortable for you. What matters most is that your prayer be a genuine respite and openness to God's presence, rather than one more item on your to-do list.
2. Find a quiet, comfortable place where you are not likely to be interrupted.
3. Turn off the television, radio, stereo, and telephone.
4. Have your Bible, a lectionary, a journal or notebook, and a pen or pencil with you.
5. If you wish, have a printed personal worship service with you.[1]

How to Begin

1. Begin by centering. Quiet your mind by listening to your breathing.
2. Visualize. See Jesus in yourself, praying along with you and perfecting your prayer. Then stretch your imagination to include church members, members of other churches, and Christians around the world.

The Discipline

1. If you are using a daily worship service, start reading through it. Read both silently and aloud and see which has more meaning for you. This might vary from day to day.
2. Do your lectionary reading in the context of your prayer. If you are using a daily prayer service, it will indicate when to turn to Scripture. If you are using the Lord's Prayer as your prayer guide, read your Scripture lessons before you begin to work your way through the prayer.
3. If for some reason you are too rushed to do the lectionary readings at your normal time, do them at one of the other prayer times.
4. Keep your journal as before.

What You Can Expect

1. Your prayer time is your living voice to God. Thus, Bible reading and prayer go together to form a conversation between you and God. A good conversationalist listens as well as speaks, does not try to dominate the conversation, and is always willing to be surprised. God is a good conversationalist. You should be also.
2. You can use set prayers if you like. The *Book of Common Worship* contains such prayers. There are also many prayer anthologies. If this way of praying seems too rigid for you, pray extemporaneously. Do not be afraid to experiment.
3. Prayer changes things. You can expect your prayers to have results. But remember that God isn't your servant. You are God's. If you see that a prayer has been answered in a special way, note it in your journal and give thanks to God.

Pitfalls

1. All the previous pitfalls still apply.
2. Don't worry about asking for something contrary to God's will. God will not grant anything contrary to God's will. Just ask and see what happens.

Appendix C

Daily Confession
as a Spiritual Discipline

A Practical Guide

APPROACHING CONFESSION

Christian confession begins with an attitude: God is love, and even God's judgment is based on love and for the sake of love. The purpose of confession is not simply to acknowledge guilt. It is to bring our life closer to God's intention for us. Confession requires a basic honesty, but more than that, it requires trust. Such a trust comes from the previous two disciplines: the study of Scripture in order to attend to God, and prayer as our response to God. Confession that is not rooted in Scripture and prayer is unlikely to be fruitful or effective. Consequently, establishing a pattern of Bible reading and prayerful responding is an important prelude to confession.

Ignatius's examen is a pattern of confession. It certainly is not the only pattern one can adopt. But it is useful, first because it is simple, and second because it begins and ends with the grace of God. Grace is the context of confession.

The pattern consists of five parts:

1. Thanking God for all that is
2. Asking God for honest discernment in recognizing sin and the willingness to abandon it
3. Reviewing the day
4. Evaluating what I have said and done
5. Deciding how I will act tomorrow

How to Prepare

1. The examen can be done at any time of day, but it is best if you are not rushed or interrupted. One possibility would be to make the examen a

121

part of your evening devotions. Another option would be to do the examen during the middle of the day, so that you can carry out any resolu-
tions during that same day. As always, do not be afraid to experiment a
bit, to discern what works best for you.

2. If you have not memorized the parts of the examen, have them in front of
    you. You might enter them in your spiritual journal, where you can refer
    to them as needed.

3. It is not strictly necessary to have your journal with you, but it is a good
    idea. You might want to record any realizations or resolutions.

How to Begin

1. Begin by centering. For the examen, you might center on whatever aspect
    or symbol of God best expresses God's compassion and guidance for you.

2. Review in your mind what it is you intend to do. The examen is not
    intended to convince you of your own sinfulness or culpability. It is not
    an exercise in masochism or self-flagellation. Rather, it is a way you can
    examine and alter your behavior.

The Discipline

1. Begin by giving thanks. In fact, the entire examen takes place in the con-
    text of thanksgiving. Say a prayer that acknowledges God's benevolence
    in creating and governing the universe and that thanks God for whatever
    good gifts have come to you this day.

2. Next ask for the particular gift of discernment in your examination. Ask
    God to help you review your day with honesty and without defensiveness
    or self-justification.

3. Then review your day (or whatever period of time has elapsed since your
    last examen). The simplest way to do this is chronological: go hour by
    hour or event by event, recalling what you said and did, and who you
    worked with and spoke to. There are other ways you can review: by
    people, by themes (e.g., when you were happy, when you were angry or
    upset, when you kept control, when you acted hastily, and so on). In this
    part of the exercise, try to refrain from judging or condemning yourself;
    simply review what you did, thought, and felt. Be aware, however, of your
    motivations as well as your actions.

4. After you have completed the review in step 3, evaluate your actions.
    Particularly note instances where you might need to ask forgiveness or
    make amends, where you need to exercise more thoughtfulness or cau-
    tion, or where you might be coming close to addictive or compulsive
    behavior.

5. Make appropriate decisions about how you will act in the immediate
    future. These should be concrete and specific. Rather than "I will be more
    thoughtful and kind" (which is, of course, laudable but not specific), your
    resolution might be "I will be more patient when my children are acting
    badly" or "I will keep my composure when my coworkers criticize me."

6. Conclude your examen with a prayer asking God to help you carry out
    your resolutions.

What You Can Expect

1. The examen is not instantaneous. Its power comes from your own willingness to be honest with yourself, and God's grace in helping you do this. You must be as patient with yourself as you would be with anyone else who is engaged in a difficult and demanding endeavor.

2. Over time, you will develop the capacity to identify those areas of your life that require amending and to take whatever steps are necessary to bring that about.

3. You might be using the examen to help with a particular issue or behavior in your life. Do not ever expect, however, that a time will come when you no longer require confession or self-examination. Dealing with your own sinfulness is a lifelong task. You will never be done with it. This does not make you a bad person. It makes you a normal person.

Pitfalls

1. Even more than Scripture study and prayer, this discipline requires dedication and perseverance in order to be fruitful. You cannot expect well-established habits or behavior patterns to disappear immediately.

2. It is inevitable that those parts of the day you will remember most clearly will be those that have produced strong feelings. Your mind will turn first to the times when you were hurt or embarrassed or to the things you have done that made you feel guilty or ashamed. Acknowledge your feelings and try to understand them, but also pay attention to the other parts of your day. You might have acted thoughtlessly or hurtfully and scarcely noticed.

3. Approach your problems one at a time. Do not try to handle all your issues at once. The first things you should attempt to correct are those that are particularly harmful to yourself or others.

4. You might not be able to sustain the examen entirely on your own. Ignatius clearly intended the one conducting the examen to be under the care of a spiritual advisor—a director or friend. A qualified and experienced spiritual director, particularly one who is familiar with the examen and its use, could be particularly helpful for you here.

Notes

Introduction

1. The World Communion of Reformed Churches' Directory of Member Churches can be found at http://www.wcrc.ch/node/164.

Chapter 1: Some Words

1. In this work, I will continue to use the Trinitarian language of *Father, Son,* and *Holy Spirit* when it is appropriate, with the understanding that these terms speak of relationship and not of gender. Nevertheless, I recognize how broken our language about God is and how careful we must be to avoid ways of speaking that falsify our understanding of God. Consequently, I will endeavor to use gender-free or gender-neutral language as much as possible.
2. Augustine of Hippo, *Confessions* X.29. In his struggle to renounce sexual activity, which he believed God was asking him to do, Augustine wrote, "You enjoin continence: give what you command, and command what you will." *The Confessions of St. Augustine* (New York: Doubleday, 1960), 256.
3. The Nicene Creed was promulgated at the Council in the year 325. The text that is in the *Book of Confessions* is not this creed, but the creed written at the Council of Constantinople in 381. The most notable difference between the two is that the Constantinopolitan Creed has a section affirming the divinity of the Holy Spirit. The creed of the Council of Nicea also contains a series of anathamas, or condemnations, that the later creed lacks.
4. For example: "The Father and I are one" (John 10:30) and "Why do you call me good? No one is good but God alone" (Mark 10:18). The first verse emphasizes the unity between Jesus and the Father, while the second distinguishes between them.
5. Albert C. Outler, ed. and trans., *Augustine: Confessions and Enchiridion,* Library of Christian Classics (Philadelphia: Westminster Press, 1955), 31.
6. The documents in the *Book of Confessions* from the Reformation Era (Scots' Confession, Heidelberg Catechism, and Second Helvetic Confession) and the seventeenth century (the Westminster documents) reflect a conflicted and polemical situation. Consequently, they make statements about other

125

churches, particularly the Roman Catholic Church, that we now find shocking and offensive. The writers were confident that they were serving God in their opposition to the Catholic Church—which was equally sure it was serving God in opposition to them. We are in a different situation today.

Chapter 2: Some Questions

1. Erik K. Erikson, *Childhood and Society* (New York and London: Norton, 1993). These conflicts are trust versus mistrust (infancy), autonomy versus shame and doubt (early childhood), initiative versus guilt (early schooling), industry versus inferiority (early schooling to puberty), identity versus role confusion (teenage years), intimacy versus isolation (early adulthood), generativity versus stagnation (mid-life), and ego integrity versus despair (later life). Gail Sheehy's *Passages: Predictable Crises of Adult Life* (New York: Ballantine, 2006) is a popular presentation of Erikson's model.
2. See Mary Wolff-Salin, *No Other Light: Points of Convergence in Psychology and Spirituality* (New York: Crossroad, 1988), 9–11.
3. Ibid., 37–38.
4. Ibid., 11, citing Carl Jung, *Two Essays on Analytical Psychology*, in *Collected Works*, vol. 7, 2nd ed. (Princeton, NJ: Princeton University Press, 1966), paragraphs 398–99.
5. Francis Kelly Nemeck and Marie Theresa Coombs, *The Spiritual Journey: Critical Thresholds and Stages of Adult Spiritual Genesis* (Collegeville, MN: Liturgical Press, 1987), 45–49.
6. Betsy Caprio and Thomas M. Hedberg, *Coming Home: A Handbook for Exploring the Sanctuary Within* (Mahwah, NJ: Paulist Press, 1986), 79–99; and *Coming Home: A Manual for Spiritual Direction* (Mahwah, NJ: Paulist Press, 1986), 7-11. This work is much more explicitly Jungian than Nemeck and Coombs' is.
7. Wolf-Salin, *No Other Light*, 76-78. In Jung's terminology, the social self is a "persona," something of a social role, even a socially imposed mask.
8. Nemeck and Coombs, *Spiritual Journey*, 66–67. They describe this process as "divergence" and "convergence": divergent possibilities are explored, leading ultimately to a convergence of appropriate or congenial options. They contrast this process, which is healthy and necessary, to drifting, in which the convergence does not occur.
9. Ibid., 101–4.

Chapter 3: Some Help

1. The word "tradition" is taken from the Latin *traditio*, meaning "to hand over."
2. Jaroslav Pelikan, *The Christian Tradition*, vol. 1, *The Emergence of the Catholic Tradition (100–600)* (Chicago: University of Chicago Press, 1971), 7. Pelikan defines *doctrine* as "what the Christian Church believes, teaches, and confesses on the basis of the Word of God" (1).
3. Presbyterian Church (U.S.A.), *Book of Common Worship* (Louisville, KY: Westminster John Knox, 1993), 517–20.
4. Ibid., 7–8.
5. Calvin, a Frenchman, had been studying at the University of Paris when he was forced to flee the city in 1533, ostensibly because he wrote or helped to write an inflammatory speech given by his friend Nicholas Cop, the rector of the university. He settled in Basel, where he published the first edition of his *Institutes of the Christian Religion*. He went to Geneva in 1536.

6. The Peace of Westphalia was a series of treaties signed in 1648 through which the religion of each state was determined by the religion of the ruling monarch. Those of other denominations were free to practice their faith in private and, to a certain extent, in public.

7. I tried to show how these four themes may be used as guides to the spiritual life in "A Map for the Journey: The Reformed Tradition as a Way of Seeking," *Insights* 122, no. 1 (Fall 2006): 3–13.

8. In his essay "The Freedom of a Christian," written in 1520, Martin Luther writes that two statements are true about Christians—the Christian is the perfectly free lord of all, and the Christian is the perfectly dutiful servant of all—and that these two statements do not contradict each other. He then goes on to distinguish between the freedom that stems from God's grace and the service that results. In both the Lutheran and the Reformed traditions—and, it seems to me, Christianity in general—service is the result of freedom, rather than the antithesis of it.

9. All three of these catechisms are structured around the Apostles' Creed, the Ten Commandments, and the Lord's Prayer.

10. There are innumerable such passages in the Pauline corpus. Romans 3:21–24 is typical: "But now, apart from law, the righteousness of God has been disclosed, and is attested by the law and the prophets, the righteousness of God through faith in Jesus Christ for all who believe. For there is no distinction, since all have sinned and fall short of the glory of God; they are now justified by his grace as a gift, through the redemption that is in Christ Jesus."

11. One can find Calvin's discussion of the three uses of the law in *Institutes of the Christian Religion* 2.7.6–16, ed. John T. McNeill, trans. Ford Lewis Battles (Philadelphia: Westminster Press, 1960), 1:354–61.

12. The actual wording of this principle in the Westminster Larger Catechism is as follows: "Where a duty is commanded, the contrary sin is forbidden; and where a sin is forbidden, the contrary duty is commanded" (*BC* 7.209, #4). The full content of this question, Q. 99, forms a hermeneutic of law—that is, a guide for how the law is to be interpreted and applied.

Interlude

1. Augustine of Hippo, *Enchiridion* 3, trans. J. F. Shaw, in Whitney J. Oakes, ed., *Basic Writings of St. Augustine*, vol. 1 (New York: Random House, 1948), 658.

2. The history of the development of creeds and creedal statements is complex. The introductions to the Nicene and Apostles' Creeds in the *Book of Confessions* give some idea of the development of these creeds, but they are necessarily simplified. For years the standard history was J. N. D. Kelly, *Early Christian Creeds*, 3rd ed. (London: Continuum, 2006). This has now been supplanted by Jaroslav Pelikan, *Credo: Historical and Theological Guide to Creeds and Confessions of Faith in the Christian Tradition* (New Haven, CT: Yale University Press, 2005).

3. Calvin included the Ten Commandments in one of his liturgies: see Bard Thompson, *Liturgies of the Western Church* (Cleveland and New York: Collins World, 1961), 191, 198, 217. The Christian Reformed Church includes the Ten Commandments as part of its regular Sunday worship.

Chapter 4: Faith

1. The Athanasian Creed is not included in the *Book of Confessions*, although it is mentioned in the Second Helvetic Confession (5.078). Also known as Quicumque Vult, after the two words beginning the Latin version, it can be

found in almost any collection of creeds, such as John Leith, ed., *Creeds of the Churches*, 3rd ed. (Atlanta: John Knox Press, 1982), 704. It can also be found in several places on the Internet.

2. This is not meant to imply that the persons of the Trinity ever work apart from each other. The fact that these works can be distinguished does not ever mean they can be separated.

3. James W. Fowler, *Stages of Faith: The Psychology of Human Development and the Quest for Meaning* (San Francisco: Harper & Row, 1981).

4. These terms as such are not used in the *Book of Confessions*. They were introduced into the vocabulary of Christian spirituality through the writings of the mysterious theologian of the fifth century usually known as Pseudo-Dionysius. One finds the idea of three stages in the Christian life even earlier, in the third-century writings of Clement of Alexandria and Origen. I am using the terms here because the concepts behind them, the descriptions of what happens at various points in one's spiritual development, are clearly present in the *Book of Confessions*, although perhaps in different ways than understood by the early and medieval church, and because contemporary writers on spirituality, both Protestant and Catholic, refer to them.

5. This distinction begins Calvin's great work, *Institutes of the Christian Religion*, where he says that which kind of knowledge has priority is difficult to determine, although "right teaching" requires that knowledge of God be taught first. Human sin obscures or obliterates what can be known about God; consequently, revelation is necessary for any knowledge that will be in aid of salvation. From this point, Calvin explores the knowledge of God the Creator, the knowledge of God the Redeemer, the way we receive the grace of Christ, and the means by which grace is transmitted. These four topics form the four "books," or major divisions, of the *Institutes*. See John Calvin, *Institutes of the Christian Religion*, ed. John T. McNeill, trans. Ford Lewis Battles (Louisville, KY: Westminster Press, 1960), 1.35-39.

6. Bullinger composed the Second Helvetic Confession in 1561 as a private exercise. It became public in 1566 when it was used in the heresy trial of Frederick the Elector and soon was adopted widely by Reformed churches in Europe. John of the Cross was imprisoned in 1577 and held until he escaped the next year. His writings did not appear until after his death.

7. There is an interesting analysis of John of the Cross in Rowan Williams, *The Wound of Knowledge*, 2nd ed. (Cambridge, MA: Crowley, 1990), 171-91, see especially p. 189, which demonstrates some of the affinities between John and Martin Luther.

8. Quoted from the *Book of Common Worship* (Louisville, KY: Westminster John Knox Press, 1993), 27.

9. These statements can be found in *BC* 3.19 (Scots Confession), *BC* 5.001–5.014 (Second Helvetic Confession), *BC* 6.001–6.010 (Westminster Confession of Faith), *BC* 7.002–7.003 (Westminster Shorter Catechism), *BC* 7.112–15 (Westminster Larger Catechism).

10. Robert M. Grant and David Tracy, *A Short History of the Interpretation of the Bible*, 2nd ed. (Minneapolis: Augsburg Fortress, 1988), provides an overview of the ways Scripture has been approached throughout the history of the church, together with a theological consideration of the nature of Scripture and revelation.

11. Doubtlessly Scripture also tells the story of God's wrath, but wrath is not the opposite of grace; it is a form of grace, just as the punishing of children is a

form of parental love. The object is not to inflict suffering; it is to correct behavior.

12. Presbyterian Church (U.S.A.), *The Book of Common Worship* (Louisville, KY: Westminster John Knox Press, 1993), 47.

13. This work is available in many editions, including *St. Ignatius of Loyola: Spiritual Exercises and Selected Works*, ed. George E. Ganss, SJ (New York: Paulist Press, 1991). Born in 1491, Ignatius was a contemporary of John Calvin. He was the founder of the Society of Jesus (colloquially known as the Jesuits). Although Ignatius was strongly opposed to the Reformation and spent a good part of his life resisting it, his *Spiritual Exercises* have been a help to Protestants and Catholics alike.

Chapter 5: Love

1. Shirley Jackson Case, *The Origins of Christian Supernaturalism* (Chicago: University of Chicago Press, 1946), 1.

2. This might in part be attributable to the strong influence of the theology of Karl Barth, who characterized God as "the one who loves in freedom." See Karl Barth, *Church Dogmatics* II/1, *The Doctrine of God*, trans. G. W. Bromiley and T. F. Torrance (Edinburgh: T. & T. Clark, 1957), 257–321.

3. The distinction between *eros* and *agape* was popularized by Anders Nygren, *Agape and Eros* (London: SPCK Press, 1953).

4. This treatise can be found in many places, including Emilie Griffin, ed., *Bernard of Clairvaux: Selected Works* (San Francisco: HarperSanFrancisco, 2005).

5. H. R. Niebuhr makes this point in *The Kingdom of God in America* (Chicago: Willett, Clark & Co., 1937), 20.

6. To paraphrase: Remember who you're talking to, don't confuse who you're talking to with anything you have made or done, and remember how to talk with the one you're talking to.

7. The earliest description of Christian worship, the *First Apology* of Justin Martyr, contains this account: "Then [after a sermon] we arise all together and offer prayers and, as we have said before, when we have concluded our prayer, bread is brought, and wine and water, and the president in like manner offers up prayers and thanksgivings with all his might; and the people assent with *Amen*, and there is the distribution and partaking by all the Eucharistic elements; and to them that are not present they are sent by the hands of the deacons." Justin, *Apology*, 1.lxvii. Quoted from Henry Bettenson and Chris Maunder, *Documents of the Christian Church*, 4th ed. (Oxford and New York: Oxford University Press, 2011), 71.

8. See Ernst Troeltsch, *The Social Teaching of the Christian Churches*, vol. 2 (New York: Harper Torchbooks, 1960), 643.

Chapter 6: Hope

1. This conclusion is based on the work of astronomer Edwin Hubble, who demonstrated that the universe is expanding. Recently, scientists have concluded that the rate of expansion is accelerating. Hubble's observation has led to a number of theories as to how the universe might end.

2. This list is not intended to be exhaustive. Many more citations could be included.

3. W. H. Auden, "For the Time Being: A Christmas Oratorio," in *Modern Poetry*, 2nd ed., ed. William Frost, vol. 7, English Masterpieces (Englewood Cliffs, NJ: Prentice Hall College Div., 1961), 215.

4. This account is quite simplified, of course, and does not do justice to the variations and nuances contained in the New Testament.
5. See N. W. Porteous, "Soul," *Interpreters' Dictionary of the Bible*, ed. George A. Buttrick et al., vol. 4 (Nashville: Abingdon Press, 1962), 428-29.
6. Among the key texts are 1 Thessalonians 4:13–18; 1 Corinthians 15; and, of course, the various Easter narratives.
7. This understanding, which was also present in the medieval church, is most explicitly set forth in the Westminster Confession of Faith in the sections "On the State of Man after Death, and of the Resurrection of the Dead" (*BC* 6.177–79) and "Of the Last Judgment" (*BC* 6.18002), and in the Westminster Larger Catechism, Q. 86–90 (*BC* 7.196–200). In this context, we also see certain features of the anti-Catholic polemic: the rejection of purgatory and the denial of the efficacy of prayers for the dead.
8. The body-soul or body-mind division has been a matter of philosophical controversy for a very long time. It is fundamental in the thinking of Rene Descartes (1596–1650), one of the most influential philosophers in the early modern era. But it has been heavily criticized, such as in Gilbert Ryle, *The Concept of Mind* (Chicago: University of Chicago Press, 2002). In this book, which was originally published in 1949, Ryle coined the phrase *the ghost in the machine* to describe Descartes' understanding of the relationship between mind and body.
9. Chap. III, *BC* 6.014–6.021. This doctrine is also discussed in some detail in the Scots Confession, chap. VIII, *BC* 3.08; the Second Helvetic Confession, chap. X, *BC* 5.052; and the Westminster Larger Catechism, Q. 12–14, *BC* 7.122–24. Other references to the doctrine appear throughout the *Book of Confessions*.
10. Swiss theologian Karl Barth gave this doctrine a thoroughgoing revision that is both respectful toward and critical of its historical shape in the Reformed tradition (Karl Barth, *Church Dogmatics* II/2, *The Doctrine of God*, trans. G. W. Bromiley and T. F. Torrance (Edinburgh: T. & T. Clark, 1957), 3-506. Barth was the primary author of the Barmen Declaration, and his thinking was one of the fundamental influences behind the Confession of 1967.
11. Strictly speaking, theodicy is the *defense* of God's power and goodness in view of the fact that there is evil in the world. The term is often used more broadly, however, to describe the mystery of evil as such.
12. Augustine of Hippo (354–430) argued that God could not have created evil because evil is not a thing but is a lack or deficiency in something that is, in and of itself, good. For example, blindness is not a thing. You will never see a pile of blindness. Blindness is actually an eye with some kind of problem. The eye itself is good.
13. Henry David Thoreau, *Walden* (1st edition published 1854), Amazon eBook, 7.
14. Some of the documents contained in the *Book of Confessions* are very critical of monasticism. Take, for example, this statement from the Westminster Confession: "Monastical vows of perpetual single life, professed poverty, and regular obedience, are so far from being degrees of higher perfection, that they are superstitious and sinful snares, in which no Christian may entangle himself" (*BC* 6.126). Such passages breathe the spirit of their times. Contemporary Christians recognize that the church, whether Protestant, Catholic, or Orthodox, owes much to the monks and that many of the most significant spiritual writers of our times have taken those very vows.

15. See Ps. 24:1, "The earth is the LORD's and all that is in it, the world, and those who live in it," and Ps. 50:10–11, "For every wild animal of the forest is mine, the cattle on a thousand hills. I know all the birds of the air, and all that moves in the field is mine."

16. Cf. "Of Holy Baptism," Second Helvetic Confession, *BC* 5.192. There are several similar passages in the *Book of Confessions*.

Appendix A: Bible Study as a Spiritual Discipline

1. A quick Internet search of "Bible reading plans" during the preparation of this manuscript produced almost one million hits. There is doubtless considerable repetition in these plans, but the point is that there are many ways of approaching Scripture reading as a regular part of one's life.

2. The Revised Common Lectionary is the result of an ecumenical collaboration known as the Consultation on Common Texts. Information on the Consultation can be found at their Internet site: http://www.commontexts.org.

3. See especially *The Book of Common Worship: Daily Prayer* (Louisville, KY: Westminster John Knox Press, 1993). The daily lectionary is also available in various forms on the Web site of the Presbyterian Church (U.S.A.): www .pcusa.org.

Appendix B: Disciplined Prayer

1. Outlines of daily personal worship services can be found in many places, including the *Book of Common Worship*. If you find these helpful, by all means use them; you can also adapt them in whatever way seems helpful to you. If you would rather not use such a service, you can use the above discussion of the Lord's Prayer as a guide for your personal prayers.

For Further Reading

On Christian Spirituality in General

Cole, Allan Hugh, Jr., ed. *A Spiritual Life: Perspectives from Poets, Prophets, and Preachers*. Louisville, KY: Westminster John Knox Press, 2011.

Downey, Michael. *Altogether Gift: A Trinitarian Spirituality*. Maryknoll, NY: Orbis Books, 2000.

Peterson, Eugene H. *Christ Plays in Ten Thousand Places: A Conversation in Spiritual Theology*. Grand Rapids, MI: Wm. B. Eerdmans Publishing Co., 2005.

On the History of Spirituality

Holt, Bradley P. *Thirsty for God: A Brief History of Christian Spirituality*, 2nd ed. Minneapolis: Augsburg Fortress, 2005.

Williams, Rowan. *The Wound of Knowledge: Christian Spirituality from the New Testament to St. John of the Cross*, 2nd rev. ed. Cambridge, MA: Crowley Publications, 1990.

On Reformed Christianity

Leith, John. *An Introduction to the Reformed Tradition: A Way of Being the Christian Community*, rev. ed. Atlanta: John Knox Press, 1981.

McKim, Donald K., ed. *Major Themes in the Reformed Tradition*. Grand Rapids, MI: Wm. B. Eerdmans Publishing Co., 1992. Reprint, Eugene, OR: Wipf & Stock, 1998.

Rice, Howard. *Reformed Spirituality: An Introduction for Believers*. Louisville, KY: Westminster/John Knox Press, 1991.

Small, Joseph D. *To Be Reformed: Living the Tradition*. Louisville, KY: Witherspoon Press, 2010.

On the *Book of Confessions*

Rogers, Jack. *Presbyterian Creeds: A Guide to the* Book of Confessions. Louisville, KY: Westminster John Knox Press, 1991.

Small, Joseph D., ed. *Conversations with the Confessions: Dialogue in the Reformed Tradition*. Louisville, KY: Geneva Press, 2005.

On Spiritual Disciplines

Cole, Allan Hugh, Jr. *The Life of Prayer: Mind, Body, and Soul.* Louisville, KY: Westminster John Knox Press, 2009.

Driskill, Joseph D. *Protestant Spiritual Exercises: Theology, History, and Practice.* Harrisburg, PA: Morehouse Publishing, 1999.

Thompson, Marjorie J. *Soul Feast: An Invitation to the Christian Spiritual Life.* Louisville, KY: Westminster John Knox Press, 2005.

Devotional Aids

Appleton, George, ed. *The Oxford Book of Prayer.* Oxford: Oxford University Press, 1985.

Book of Common Worship: Daily Prayer. Louisville, KY: Westminster John Knox Press, 1993.

Index

CPSIA information can be obtained at www.ICGtesting.com
Printed in the USA
BVOW04s2105310314

349327BV00002B/52/P